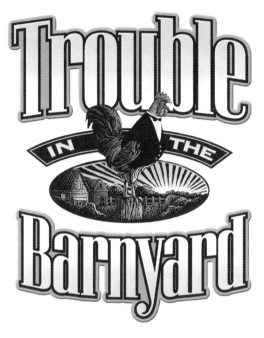

Trouble IN THE Barnyard

Dr. Earl Carter

To Pastor Kith

Dr. Earl Carter Sr.

WINEPRESS WP PUBLISHING

Printed in the United States of America

Published by WinePress Publishing,
PO Box 428, Enumclaw, WA 98022.

Unless otherwise noted all scriptures are taken from the King
James Version of the Bible.

Verses marked TLB are taken from The Living Bible, Copyright ©
1971 owned by assignment by Illinois Regional Bank N.A. (as
trustee). Used by permission of Tyndale House Publishers, Inc.,
Wheaton, Illinois 60189. All rights reserved

ISBN 1-57921-250-6

Library of Congress Catalog Card Number: 99-65699

Acknowledgments

I'd like to thank God for this opportunity to be used of Him to write such a book which hopefully will bring healing and restoration to marriages and families.

I'd like to thank my wife Beverly and my children Dominique and E.J. for giving up so much of their quality time with me so that I could complete this book.

I'd like to thank the entire Christ Ministries family for their loving support, along with my secretary, Shonna, for her spirit of servitude and administrative excellence.

Finally, I'd like to thank Alex Almeyda, MD. for the wonderful foreword that greatly contributed to the message of this book.

Contents

Foreword

◆ ◆ ◆ ◆ ◆

They hate him who reproves in the gate and they abhor him who speaks with integrity. (Amos 5:10)

When a man of God speaks the truth from God's Word, he usually brings on firestorms of protest and criticism. The storm comes from both those who *oppose* the Word and also from those who only preach the Word *part way*. My friend and neighbor, Dr. Earl Carter, Sr. is in for a firestorm, and I have told him so.

But it's a storm that needs to be raised. As a Florida licensed physician, psychiatrist and Christian counselor, I have observed the mayhem in the lives of my private patients, in their families and even in churches. Many of these imbalances result from boundary issues, interpersonal abuses, over-assertiveness or non-assertiveness, enmeshing roles, etc. All of these factors undermine marital relations and the stability of the home. Pills don't help because these problems are rooted in the *spiritual* realm.

The subject matter of Reverend Carter's book *Trouble In The Barnyard* takes an insightful look at the problem of role usurpation within the male-female relationship.

Deuteronomy 22:5 speaks to women not wearing the clothes of a man and is an injunction against the sexes not assuming gender roles that are not theirs. The one who does so is a usurper. . . .

For millennia, the Satan-inspired tactic of usurpation has been to challenge and attempt to topple God's order of things. The Bible speaks of Satan attempting to usurp God's throne in eternity past. In Eden, Satan attempted to have Eve and her husband Adam usurp the omniscience of God in order to "be as God." Jezebel, the Queen of Israel, usurped her husband's authority in order to steal a vineyard from its rightful owners. In the times of Amos, women were literally characterized by God as "cows of Bashan" for being not only unjust too often, but also for treating their men as servile providers of wine. Severe divine punishment was decreed (Amos 4:1–3.)

In today's homes and churches, the order between males and females has been lost in a fog of egalitarianism. Women seem to be commanding or lording over men from home as well as from the pulpit. There is disrespect for the man, disregard for his leadership and disdain for his authority. Women have become usurpers of men. No longer subject, no longer modest, no longer willing to follow. Women have a new militancy which says, "You've come a long way, Baby!" But, where in God's plan, are they going?

In all fairness, men too have become usurpers of God; doing as they will, intruding into areas of life that don't belong to them, abdicating their responsibilities to women and their duty to train their children in the Word of God. They want power, but not responsibility. They leave their homes and families in droves, creating a vacuum that women attempt to fill.

Satan does not want God to be man's covering. He does not want man to be woman's covering. This leaves the *children,* the objects of his most fervent hatred, with no covering at all. Dr. Carter's premise for his book, *Trouble In The Barnyard* is based on honoring the *divinely engineered* differences God intended for the sexes and honoring also His reasons for making it so. When home and church failed to do so, all kinds of social and spiritual errors will result.

After years of treating individuals, couples and families, I am convinced that usurpation of gender roles can lead to anger, irritability, rage, depression, anxiety and numerous other psychological and psychiatric symptoms.

This book is likely to elicit a virulent backlash by those who subscribe to feminist agendas in society and in churches. Most churches are so afraid of this backlash they avoid the subject altogether. However, we can no more ignore such scriptures as 1 Corinthians 11:1-3, 11:12-16; 1 Corinthians 14:33 and 1 Timothy 2:11-14 than we can ignore John 3:16.

Does the present-day instability of the family unit have anything to do with the disregard toward the God-given order of things? If the same process is occurring in the churches, is it any surprise the Church has been impotent to help keep homes together?

What is the rightful place of the man, the woman and their children in today's home? Whatever it is, it should not be usurpation of another's role, process or authority. It should be obedience to God's plan.

I am pleased to write the foreword for Dr. Carter's book. He "reproves at the gate," as the Prophet Amos said—and it must be said. For the usurpers of today have laid waste the family, and only adherence to God's principles can restore it. Dr. Carter has spoken with integrity, casting aside all personal and political considerations. I find his message powerful and compelling, and I am sure the reader will too.

ALEXANDER D. ALMEYDA, M.D.
President, Sebring Psychiatry P.A.
Member, American Association of
Christian Counselors

Introduction

very now and then a strange phenomenon occurs down
on the farm: a hen will begin to crow like a rooster. When
that happens, there's trouble in the barnyard.

This book is a Biblically based metaphorical account of the
divinely ordered system of headship in the home. In this day
and time, the home is under attack from within and without. It
is high time for the Church to give some clear direction on the
subject. Relationship gives meaning to life, and the home is
the foundation of a society; if the home is destroyed, so goes
the society.

God has established only three institutions: the home, government, and the church. Those three institutions form the basic building blocks of a sane and well-ordered society.

Family

The first institution God founded was the family. The family, according to Genesis 2:18-25, was to provide a haven for its members as they prepare to enter society and to serve God and their fellowman.

Government

Human government was founded by God (Genesis 9:4-7; 10:5; Romans 13:18) for the purpose of protecting man from those depraved individuals who either had not learned in their family—or refused to obey—God's principles of respect for others and their property, so necessary to civilization.

Church

The church was instituted many centuries later because the family and government had both failed. I believe in some ways the church has failed also. The church has failed to communicate the principles of God concerning the family. For instance, many churches try to stay away from the question of headship because the subject is politically incorrect. They give in to the 50/50 mentality of the world. But Romans 13:1-8 says, "Let every man be subject to the higher power." In a world of women's rights and domestic violence from both sides, even Christian marriages are struggling because many do not understand the subject of headship. Some say we don't need headship, rather, we need *same-ship*. As a result we have *insane-ship*. The scripture lets us know in 1 Corinthians 14:33 that "God is not the author of confusion, but of peace." And in 1 Corinthians 14:40 Paul says, "Let all things be done decently and in order."

Headship is God's design to reduce problems by having one person in the leadership position in every relationship. The concept of headship is not an unusual one. It's recognized as the normal way of doing things in organizations from major corporations and government to community organizations; from great countries to small primitive tribes. When organizations are left without a head, they deteriorate rapidly in a state of confusion. I must point out, brothers, that although headship is a position of power and authority, it is not a position of dictatorship but a servant's position, designed to serve those you love by taking the responsibility for their well-being.

Headship is not acceptable when we are bent on having our own way. If we are honest, we all have a problem with headship; whether with mere man or the Holy Son of God, Jesus Christ— the perfect Head of the Church. Disrespect to headship of any kind will always breed conflict.

Trouble In The Barnyard was born out of my concern for the home and the family. What I am witnessing is in the church as well as the world—the world is out of order and so is the church relative to this subject. Once I heard that every now and then a strange phenomenon occurs in the barnyard. A hen will begin to crow like a rooster. When that hen starts sounding like a rooster, the farmer must remove that hen from the barnyard— and usually the hen becomes dinner for that night! It is said that the farmer must do this because the hen disrupts the order in the barnyard and all the other hens are drawn to her and thus the production of eggs and new chickens cease.

I also have heard that every now and then, there is a rooster that pecks on the hen for no reason at all, and so the farmer must also remove him from the barnyard. My first experience with domestic violence was in my home, when my father and mother were engaged in fighting one another. It lasted all of my childhood. The marriage couldn't last and didn't, because they were not Christians.

Of course Christians have problems too, but you will have a better chance sustaining a marriage when Christian principles are at heart.

Yet after becoming a Christian and being excited about my new life in Christ, I saw something that disturbed me greatly. One night after church, a Christian man and I were outside talking about the goodness of the Lord. All of a sudden, here comes his wife—a little lady about 5 feet. tall—who disgracefully said to her husband, a robust 6-footer, "Let's go Henry!"

And this giant of a man did a one-two hop almost running, and left Jesus and me standing there. That disturbed me greatly. So I asked some of the members of the church why she spoke to him in that way and treated him so badly. They replied, "because she has money and he's henpecked." That never left me, and it's been almost thirty years ago. There are so many examples I could give, but I think you know what I mean. Without any further explanation, let's get started.

PART ONE

HEN-PECKED

HUSBAND

Part One

Hen-Pecked Husband

But there was none like unto Ahab, which did sell himself to work wickedness in sight of the Lord, whom Jezebel his wife stirred up. (1 Kings chapters 18 and 19, 1 Kings 21:19, 2 Kings 9:30-37)

Ahab and Jezebel

King Ahab of Israel was a weak, henpecked man. He was dominated by his wife, Jezebel, who loved to stir up wickedness. She was a woman who chose not to recognize her husband's God and did all that *she* wanted to do. Ahab should have led his people by doing right, but he chose to listen to Jezebel instead of listening to God.

But that's ancient history. What do Ahab and Jezebel have to do with us now? Well, look around you. It seems as if the spirit of Jezebel is alive and thriving, both in today's society and in the church.

Look at the symptoms: Men are having a very difficult time dealing with disobedient wives. They're becoming weak and apathetic, or are getting so frustrated they resort to verbal or physical abuse.

I can hear you thinking, *You may be right, but what am I supposed to do about it?* We'll get to the solution as you read further on.

First, though, we must recognize the source of the disobedience. As a Christian, you well know that "we wrestle not against flesh and blood." We are in warfare "against principalities, against powers, against the rulers of darkness of this world, against spiritual wickedness in high places" (Ephesians 6:12). One of the principalities is the Jezebel Spirit. When we speak of Jezebel, we are identifying the source in our society of obsessive sensuality, unbridled witchcraft, and hatred for male authority.

I see that spirit working strongly in the world and also in the church. Jezebel caused over ten million Hebrews, all but seven thousand faithful souls, to bow to Baal and forsake the covenant. Now the Jezebel-controlled Church is causing us to forsake the

God-ordained patriarchal order for a system that causes great destruction in families.

For instance, I told you about Henry, who hopped at his wife's command. To me, that was a Jezebel-controlled moment. Wherever you see men controlled or manipulated by their wives, you're seeing men under the spell of the Jezebel Spirit working through their wives.

Some twenty years ago, a friend of mine married a seemingly nice church-going woman. As expected, in the beginning everything was coming up roses, but all of a sudden, things changed. They started fighting regularly. He told me as well as others that he had made a mistake by marrying this young lady. We asked him why he felt that way, and he told us that she was too mean and controlling. So we advised him to give the marriage a chance to develop. We felt they just needed time to adjust since they were only newlyweds.

He took our advice and tried to make it work, but it didn't because he didn't get any help from his local church. She was one of the leaders, a dominant force, in the church, therefore no one felt the need—or had the courage—to correct her.

One day he told me that he was miserable and wanted a divorce. I tried to talk him out of it by attempting to frighten him by telling him "what God hath joined together, let no man put asunder," and that if he were to marry again he would be living in adultery and may go to hell. (That was my understanding at the time, but my understanding has changed greatly since then).

The brother told me that he was already in hell and left the marriage and God for almost 20 years. He just recently came back to church, thank God for that!

Marriage should be a wonderful experience, but in cases like his, it's not. When the hen acts like the rooster, you have trouble in the barnyard. It wreaks havoc in the family, and in the church, and pastors are not immune to its effects.

Recently at the National Convocation of the Church of God in Christ in Memphis, I was selling my books and was shocked to see so many of our men of the cloth controlled by their wives. One man said to me, "I like your book *No Apology Necessary,* but I have to see if my wife likes your book before I can buy it." Yes, he said "I don't buy anything without my wife liking it."

Another man came to the table and said, "I like your book, but I have to go to my wife to get the ten dollars."

Shocked, I replied, "You mean to tell me that you don't have ten dollars, and you have to go to your wife and get it?"

Embarrassed he said, "Yes, my wife handles all the money." Now don't get me wrong, sometimes it's good that the woman handles the money allocated for the house to pay the bills, etc. But not *all* of the money. The husband should always have some money on him, and hopefully more than ten dollars!

I was invited to speak at a meeting in another city. Everything was planned, plane ticket and hotel had been reserved, and everything was on schedule. But one morning I received a phone call from the pastor, who nervously informed me that the meeting had to be canceled. I asked why and if I had done anything wrong. He told me no. I then remembered I had told him my financial arrangement, which at the time was fine.

Later on at the Convocation I was informed of the real reason for the cancellation—his wife was unhappy with the financial arrangement. When the pastor and his wife were respectfully confronted about the cancellation by one of the co-sponsors of the meeting, the wife did all of the talking and the pastor said nothing.

The young co-sponsor then turned to his wife and said, "We're out of here." He and his family left that church because of the dominance of the pastor's wife. That young man also stated that he couldn't stay where the pastor was being controlled by his wife. "And Jezebel stirred Ahab to do evil in the sight of the Lord."(See 1 Kings 21:25.) Jezebel will not dwell with anyone unless she can control and dominate the relationship.

Zombies Among Us

That same pastor came to my table to get his copy of *No Apology Necessary* with glazed eyes that looked weird, like a zombie. He lethargically said, "I want a book." At that point, I knew that brother was under the witchcraft spell of Jezebel, as so many others are. That's when I knew I had to write this book, *Trouble In The Barnyard*. The man walked away ashamed of himself. He couldn't even look me in the eye. Could it be that his wife knew something about him that's too embarrassing for others to know? Or maybe she would openly embarrass him in the church.

Witchcraft, you see, is simply manipulation, domination and intimidation. It's the ability to get someone to do something they don't want to do out of fear. Fear of being found out, fear of being alone, fear of other people's opinions—witchcraft works through fear.

Chapter One

Pecking Too Hard—
Domestic Violence

PART ONE: HEN-PECKED HUSBANDS

Spousal abuse is a problem that does occur in Christian marriages. But it's not all men abusing their wives. Some times it's women who abuse their husbands and this abuse, be it physical or mental, is just as wrong as when the wife is the victim. From an article entitled "Men: The Secret Victims of Domestic Violence" comes some interesting statistics about battered men:[1]

Violence against women is clearly a problem of national importance, but has anyone ever asked how often men are beaten by women? The unfortunate fact is that men are the victims of domestic violence at least as often as women. While the very idea of men being beaten by their wives runs contrary to many of our deeply ingrained beliefs about men and women, female violence against men is a well-documented phenomenon almost completely ignored by both the media and society.

Violence takes various forms. There is no question that since men are, on average, bigger and stronger than women, they can do more damage in a fist fight. However, according to Professors R. L. McNeely and Coramae Richey Mann, "the average man's size and strength are neutralized by guns and knives, boiling water, bricks, fireplace pokers and baseball bats." In fact, a 1984 study of 6,200 cases of reported domestic assault found the 86% of female-on-male violence involved weapons while only 25% of male-on-female violence did.

According to many women's rights advocates, female violence against men—if it exists at all—is purely a self-defense response to male violence. Several studies, however, show that women initiate about one quarter of all domestic assaults, men initiate another quarter, and the remaining half are classified as "mutual." Other researchers, attempting to discredit the findings on men as victims, claim that since women are physically weaker and do less damage, only "severe assaults" should be compared. The results of that analysis show men are only slightly more likely to initiate the violence. Overall, Dr. Straus found that whether the analysis is based on all assaults, or is focused exclusively on dangerous assaults, "about as many women as men attack a spouse who has not hit them during a one year period." Clearly, then, the claim that women's violence is purely "self-defense" doesn't hold water.

So I ask, what are women thinking about if they are physically attacking their husbands? They certainly are not thinking about Ephesians 5:33 which tells her to reverence her husband. The word "reverence" comes from the Greek word *phobeo* from which we get our English word "phobia." Just like in the Greek, our word means "to fear." According to Vine's Expository Dictionary of Biblical Words it's used in the passive voice in the New Testament of reverential fear on the part of a wife for a husband.[2] The word for "reverence" used in Ephesians 5:33, is the same word translated "fear" in 1 Peter 2:17, "Honour all men. Love the brotherhood. *Fear* God. Honour the king." In Revelation 19:5, "And a voice came out of the throne, saying, Praise our God, all ye his servants, and ye that *fear* him, both small and great." Wives are to respect their husbands with the same kind of respect they have for God. So, a woman who beats up her husband isn't showing him respect and therefore, isn't showing God respect either.

Remember Proverbs 11:29? "He that troubleth his own house shall inherit the wind: and the fool shall be servant to the wise of heart." This applies to wives as well. The woman who abuses her husband brings trouble upon her own house and she's considered a fool who needs to be controlled by someone who is wise. A wife's mistreatment of her husband is inexcusable.

How foolish it is for a wife to abuse the husband she chose! Even if he's not living up to his role as lover, protector, and provider, abusing him certainly won't make him become what she thinks he should be. She is driving away her love, her protection, and her provision. How much sense does that make? She's certainly troubling her own house. She is a fool. I didn't say that, the Bible says it. Argue with the Word of God. She needs help and deliverance.

"The Husband Abusers," an article by Gary Thomas in *New Man Magazine*,[3] speaks to the problem of going public with this issue and offers a few suggestions for the control of the problem:

> The two biggest challenges to addressing the is-
> sues of husband abuse continue to be shame and

unbelief: the shame of the male victims and our society's unbelief that men actually could be recipients of domestic violence.

After *New Man* published a cover story on domestic abuse against women last May,[4] the editors were shocked to find themselves inundated with letters from anonymous husbands begging the magazine to tell the other side of the story. A survey of these men's letters suggests that abused men are pleading with the church to take their plight seriously. One anonymous man said, "Our society must realize that some women can be just as cruel and violent in the family relationship as some men."

Susan Bursztynsky urges churches and pastors to take a more proactive position on the problem of all spousal abuse. "Everyone has to take a coordinated stance that violence in any form will not be tolerated," she says. "We need to make synagogues and churches 'victim friendly.'"

How do we do this? "Address domestic violence in sermons," Bursztynsky urges. "When we are silent on it we open ourselves up to a situation in which the spouse says, 'The pastor never talks about it so it must be OK.' Domestic violence needs to be discussed in Bible studies and in situations where men and women are separated." She even encourages churches to put up posters in rest rooms to let victims know there is a place they can go for help.

If churches are truly going to help, they should consider consulting professionals who are familiar with the problem. One man, whom we'll call "Craig," went from being abused by his father to being physically abused by his wife (who was bigger and stronger than he was). After literally being beat up, Craig ran to a friend who told *New Man*, "I did the most stupid thing in my life. I thought that my church would be able to help him. Wrong! All they did was pray for him, and they told him to go back. This man was crying out and all they did was send him back! Didn't they see he was not strong enough to stop her or leave her by himself?"

Some pastors or counselors may treat husband abuse less seriously than wife abuse, but abused husbands should not give up. There are Christian professionals who are willing to help. For instance, in their counseling of couples, David and Claudia Arp use a unique tool to help husbands and wives deal with their anger more productively. "All of us

get angry." Arp points out. "Our culture is stressful. Unfortunately, most couples don't know how
to process anger constructively, so my wife and I
use a contract that was brought to our attention
by Drs. David and Vera Mace." The contract has
three parts:

1.   One of the spouses must be up front and com-
municative as soon as they recognize their own
anger. "It simply means agreeing to say at the
outset, 'I'm beginning to get angry with you right
now.'" Arp believes this verbalizing helps to bring
anger out into the open and often can "nip it in
the bud" right there.

2.   Couples should agree ahead of time that "I am
not going to vent my anger on you. Anger is my
problem, not yours."

3.   The final step is a plea for understanding and
help. Spouses should be open and vulnerable
enough to say, "Help me process this anger so that
it becomes a positive in thisrelationship. Help
me figure out the cause."

The Arps encourage couples to actually sign this contract so that when heated moments arise, one can remind the other, "Remember that contract. We're not supposed to respond with violence."

If you're facing husband abuse, consider the Arps' plan for handling anger—your own and your wife's. It could be helpful to seriously consider writing your own "anger contract". Also, take to heart one woman's words about husbands being inattentive. Are you unwittingly setting up an abusive event by your own passivity or lack of communication? She calls her husband "a master at sarcasm and passive-aggressive remarks that leave me confused." You can't control your wife, but you can control your own communication.

One man has found help by sharing his struggle in a small group at his church. Though he admits it can be difficult to seek help for fear of "being looked at as a wimp or worse," he points out that "people probably already know what is happening. You can't hide it from people who are around both of you." Find the courage to admit this, and share your burden with another brother. Remember, he probably already knows anyway but may be too embarrassed himself to raise the issue.

In conclusion, whether the wife is being battered or the husband is being abused, the perpetrator is in the wrong. God set up a beautiful system when he instituted marriage. He did not intend for either party, the wife or the husband, to end up being mistreated in the relationship. Marriage is supposed to be a picture of the wonderful union between Christ and the Church—the husband representing Christ and the wife representing His body, the Church. Christ and the Church don't beat up on one another; neither should the husband and the wife.

Chapter Two

Willie Lynch and the Jezebel Connection

Once at our holy convocation in Memphis, we had a speaker from Africa who told a story of a young African boy who was caught stealing. The boy was asked, "Why did you steal?"

He answered, "It's in my bones. My father was a thief."

This boy believed he could do nothing more than his father had done. His upbringing was all he knew. In studying the problem of gender role and the Jezebel Spirit, I have come to the conclusion that what the Black family is dealing with is "generational perpetuality" of its legacy of forced fractured relationships.

Although slavery had a profound effect on American society as a whole and on the African-American subculture in particular; the most profound and damaging influence of slavery was perpetrated upon the Black family.

In his book *Chains and Images of Psychological Slavery*,[5] clinical psychologist Dr. Na'im Akbar, Ph.D. states:

> The family is the very foundation of healthy, constructive, personal and community life. Without a strong family, individual life and community life are likely to become very unstable. The destruction or damage to the Black family was accomplished by destroying marriage, fatherhood, and motherhood.

To further prove his point, Dr. Akbar continues:

> Slavery was "legally" ended in excess of 100 years ago, but the over 300 years experienced in its brutality and unnaturalness constituted a severe psychological and social shock to the minds of African-Americans. This shock was so destructive to natural life processes that psychologists and sociologists have failed to attend to the persistence of problems (that plague the) current generation of African-Americans. And although we are 5–6 generations (away from slavery) in both our social and mental lives, (it's clear to see

that these current problems) clearly have their roots in slavery. Only the historian has given proper attention to the shattering realities of slavery, and he has dealt with it only as descriptive of past events.

K.L. Clark, m.p., in the book *The Development of Consciousness of Self*,[6] observes that most social scientists would object to a discussion of slavery as a cause of contemporary behavior because it happened "too long ago." Clark identifies the origin of this objection in the nineteenth-century conceptions of science, articulated by the British philosophers Locke and Hume, and practiced by the scientific giant, Isaac Newton. Clark observes:

> In the Newtonian scheme of things, "a body at rest remains at rest unless acted upon by some external force." The behavior (movement) of things was thought to be the consequence of some antecedent and external event . . . Newtonian conceptions of absolute time and space have so conditioned many of us that it is impossible for us to conceive of events that have occurred "long in the past" (e.g. slavery) as having as much effect in determining present behavior as those events of relatively "recent" occurrence.

Clark, in this monumental piece, argues that more than any other event, slavery shaped the mentality of present African-Americans.

So what has all this to do with the Black family today? Plenty. If behavior is indeed understood as the consequence of some antecedent and external event, and slavery is known to have indeed been an antecedent and external event in relation to today's Black family, then a study of what effect slavery had on the Black family is in order. An understanding of how the Black family was funneled through the sieve of slavery will bring into focus some of the issues faced, fought over, and many times failed, in the Black family today.

Listen as Dr. Akbar quotes William Goodell (1853) as he describes the institution of marriage as it was viewed by slaveholders:

> The slave has no rights, of course, he or she cannot have the right of a husband or a wife. The slave is a chattel and chattels do not marry. (Chattel is a thing you own.) The slave is not ranked among sentient beings, but among things, and things are not married . . .
>
> The obligations of marriage are evidently inconsistent with the conditions of slavery, and cannot be performed by a slave. The husband promises to protect his wife and provide for her. The wife

promises to be the helpmeet of her husband. They mutually promise to live with and cherish each other, til parted by death. But what can such promises by slaves mean? The legal relation of master and slave renders them void. It forbids the slave to protect even himself. It clothes his master with authority to bid him inflict deadly blows on the woman he as sworn to protect. It prohibits his possession of any property where-with to sustain her. . . . It gives the master unlimited control and full possession of her own person, and forbids her, on pains of death, to resist him, if he drags her to his bed! It severs the plighted pair at the will of their masters, occasionally or forever.

Dr. Akbar comments on Goodell's description thusly:

These quotes graphically illustrate the ultimate meaninglessness of marriage for the slaves. Even under circumstances where the marriage ties were not arbitrarily violated, the very condition of slavery contradicted much about the vital and fundamental condition of marriage.

This is how slave marriages were actually looked upon by the masters—as a charade, a sham, a hoax. At its most elementary level, one can already begin to see that, if the institution of marriage was left to go on this way for long, the participants themselves would likely begin to understand the meaninglessness of their own belief in marriage.

Let Dr. Akbar quickly speak to the issue of what should be done with our new knowledge:

> The objective should not be to cry stale tears for the past, nor to rekindle old hatreds for past injustices. Instead, we should seek to enlighten our paths of today by yesterday. We should also understand that slavery should be viewed as a starting point for understanding the African-American psyche, and not as an end point.

To give you a deeper understanding of the intentional damage perpetrated upon the Black family, let us examine one more historical document here. The deception and the cycle of destruction for the Black family was set in motion long ago and is graphically described in a speech entitled *On How to Make a Slave*, delivered on the banks of the James River in 1712 by William Lynch, a white slave owner.[7]

On How to Make a Slave
By William Lynch

Gentlemen, I greet you here on the banks of the
James River in the year of our Lord one thousand
seven hundred and twelve. First, I shall thank you,
the gentlemen of the colony of Virginia for bringing me here. I am here to help you solve some of
your problems with slaves. Your invitation
reached me on my modest plantation in the West
Indies where I have experimented with some of
the newest and still the oldest methods for the
control of slaves. Ancient Rome would envy us if
my program is implemented. As our boat sailed
south on the James River, named for our illustri-
ous King, whose version of the Bible we cherish,
I saw enough to know that your problem is not
unique. While Rome used cords of wood as crosses
for standing human bodies along its old highways
in great numbers you are here using the tree and
rope on occasion.

I caught a whiff of a dead slave hanging from a
tree a couple of miles back. You are not only losing
valuable stock by hangings, you are having upris-
ings, slaves are running away, your crops are
sometimes left in the fields for too long for

maximum profit, you suffer occasional fires, your
animals are killed. Gentlemen, you know what
your problems are; I do not need to elaborate. I
am not here to enumerate your problems, I am
here to introduce you to a method of solving them.

In my bag here, I have a fool proof method for
controlling your Black slaves. I guarantee everyone of you that if installed correctly, it will control
the slaves for at least 300 years. My method is
simple. Any member of your family or your over-
seer can use it.

I have outlined a number of differences among the
slaves: and I take these differences and make them
bigger. I use fear, distrust, and envy for control purposes. These methods have worked on my modest
plantation in the West Indies and it will work
throughout the South. Take this simple little list of
differences and think about them On top of my list
is "Age" but it is there only because it starts with
"A". The second is "Color" or shade. There is intelligence, size, sex, size of plantations, status of plantation, attitude of owners, whether the slaves live
in the valley, or a hill, East, West, North, South,
have fine hair or coarse hair, or is tall or short.
Now that you have a list of differences, I shall give

you an outline of action, but before that I shall assure you that distrust is stronger than trust, and envy is stronger than adulation, respect or admiration. The Black slave after receiving this indoctrination shall carry on and will become self re-fueling and self-generating for hundreds of years, maybe thousands.

Don't forget—you must pitch the old Black male against the young Black male, and the young Black male against the old Black male. You must use the dark-skinned slaves against the light-skinned slaves, and the light-skinned slaves versus the dark-skinned slaves. You must use the female versus the male, and the male versus the female. You must also have all your white servants and overseers distrust all Blacks, but it is necessary that your slaves trust and depend on us. They must love, respect, and trust only us.

The Systematic Physical Breaking and Psychological Reversing Process

. . . Break the will to resist. Now the breaking process is the same for both the horse and the Black, only slightly varying in degrees. But as we said before, there is an art in long range economic planning.

You must keep your eye and thoughts on the female and the offspring of the horse and the Black.

A brief discourse in offspring development will shed light on the key to sound economic principles. Pay little attention to the generation of original breaking but concentrate on future generations. Therefore, if you break the female mother, she will break the offspring in its early years of development, and when the offspring is old enough to work, she will deliver it up to you for her normal female productive tendencies will have been lost in the original breaking process.

For example, take the case of the wild stud horse, a female horse, and an already infant horse and compare the breaking process with two captured Black males in their natural state, a pregnant Black woman with her infant offspring. Take the stud horse, break him for limited containment. Completely break the female horse until she becomes gentle whereas you or anybody else can ride her in comfort. Breed the mare and the stud until you have the desired offspring. Then you can turn the stud to freedom until you need him again. Train the female horse whereby she will eat out of your hand, and she will, in turn, train the infant horse to eat out of your hand also.

When it comes to breaking the uncivilized Black, use the same process, but vary the degree and step up the pressure so as to do a complete reversal of the mind. Take the meanest and most restless Black, strip him of his clothes in front of the remaining male Blacks, the female, and the infant Black. Tar and feather him, tie each leg to a different horse faced in opposite directions, set him afire, and beat both horses to put him apart in front of the remaining Blacks. The next step is to take a bull whip and beat the remaining Black males to the point of death in front of the female and infant. Don't kill them, but put the fear of God in them, for they can be useful for future breeding.

The Breaking Process of the African Woman

Then take the female, run a series of tests on her to see if she will submit to your desires willingly. Test her in every way because she is the most important factor for good economics. If she shows any sign of resistance in submitting completely to your will, do not hesitate to use the bull whip on her to extract the last bit of bitch out of her. Take care not to kill her, for, in doing so, you spoil good economics. When in complete submission, she will train offspring in the early years to submit to labor when they become of age.

Understanding is the best thing. Therefore, we shall go deeper into this area of the subject matter concerning what we produced here in this breaking process of the female Black. We have reversed the relationships. In her natural uncivilized state she would have a strong dependency on the uncivilized Black male, and she would have a limited protective tendency toward her man, independent male offspring and would raise the female offspring to be dependent like her. Nature had provided for this type of balance. We reversed nature by burning and pulling one civilized Black apart and bull-whipping the other to the point of death—all in her presence. By her being left alone, unprotected, with the male image destroyed, the ordeal caused her to move from her psychological dependent state to a frozen independent state. In the frozen psychological state of independence she will raise her male and female offspring in reverse roles. For fear of the young male's life, she will psychologically train him to be mentally weak and dependent but physically strong.

Because she has become psychologically independent, she will train her female offspring to be
psychologically independent. What have you got?
You've got the Black woman out front and the Black
man behind and scared. This is a perfect situation
for sound sleep and economics.

Before the breaking process, we had to be alertly
on guard at all times. Now we can sleep soundly,
for, out of frozen fear, his woman stands guard for
us, he cannot get past her early infant slave molding process. He is a good tool, now ready to be tied
up to the horse at a tender age.

By the time a Black boy reaches the age of six-
teen, he is soundly broken in and ready for a long
life of sound and efficient work and the reproduction of a unit of good labor force.

Continually, through the breaking of uncivilized
savage Blacks, by throwing the Black female
savage into a frozen psychological state of inde-
pendency, by killing of the protective male image,
and by creating a submissive dependent mind of
the Black male savage, we have created an orbiting cycle that turns on its own axis forever, unless
a phenomenon occurs and reshifts the position

of the male and female savages. We show what
we mean by example. Take the case of two economic slave units and examine them closely.

The Negro Marriage Unit

We breed two Black males with two Black females.
Then we take the Black males away from them
and keep them moving and working. Say the one
Black female bears another Black female and the
other bears a Black male. Both Black females,
being without influence of the Black male image,
frozen with an independent psychology, will raise
their offspring into reverse positions. The one
with the female offspring will teach her to be like
herself, independent and negotiable (we negotiate with her, through her, by her, and negotiate
at her will). The one with the Black male offspring, she being frozen with a subconscious fear
for his life, will raise him to be mentally dependent and weak, but physically strong—in other
words, body over mind.

Warning Possible Interloping Negatives

Earlier, we talked about the non-economic good
of the horse and the Black in their wild or natural

state; we talked about the principle of breaking and tying them together for orderly production; furthermore, we talked about paying particular attention to the female savage and her offspring for orderly future planning; then, more recently we stated that, by reversing the positions of the male and female savages, we had created an orbiting cycle that turns on its own axis forever, unless a phenomenon occurred and reshifted the positions of the male and female savages.

Our experts warned us about the possibility of this phenomenon occurring, for they say that the mind has a strong drive to correct and recorrect itself over a period of time if it can touch some substantial original historical base; and they advised us that the best way to deal with this phenomenon is to shave off the brute's mental history and create a multiplicity of phenomena of illusions, so that each illusion will twirl in its own orbit, something similar to floating balls in a vacuum.

This creation of a multiplicity of phenomena of illusions entails the principles of cross-breeding the Black and the horse as we stated above, the purpose of which is to create a diversified division of labor, the results of which is the severance of the points of the original beginnings for each sphere illusion. Since we feel that the subject matter may get more complicated as we proceed in laying down our economic plan concerning the purpose, reason, and effect of cross-breeding horses and Blacks, we shall lay down the following definitional terms for future generations:

1. Orbiting cycle means a thing turning in a given path.

2. Axis means that upon which or around which a body turns.

3. Phenomenon means something beyond ordinary conception and inspires awe and wonder.

4. Multiplicity means a great number.

5. Sphere means globe.

6. Cross-breeding a horse means taking a horse and breeding it with an ass and you get a dumb backward longhead mule that is not reproductive nor productive by itself.

7. Cross-breeding Blacks means taking so many drops of good white blood and putting them into as many Black women as possible, varying the drops by the various tones that you want, and then letting them

break with each other until the circle of colors appear as you desire.

Reading that speech did several things for me. It changed my understanding and also proved my thesis in *No Apology Necessary*. First, I understand why we Blacks as a people can't seem to get together and create a networking system like other races. However, consider Isaiah 19:2, "I will set Egyptians against Egyptian: Egyptian woman against Egyptian man." This could not have happened except God permitted it.

Second, I now understand what happened to our women, and why they are the way they are. They actually made the Black woman a secret slave master's assistant. Wow! Slave master's assistants! Remember in the speech, before the breaking process, the masters had to be on guard at all times. Now they could sleep soundly for out of frozen fear the Black woman stood guard for them. The Black child could not get past her early infant slave-molding process and would grow to become a good tool, ready to be tied up to the horse at a tender age.

With the male image of protection destroyed, the Black man was reduced to strenuous work and stud service, like a horse. This is why we have so many or our men, who seem to strive on the reputation of being strong-armed studs. That attitude comes from slavery. The man who gets a woman pregnant and leaves her to get another woman pregnant ends up with babies all over town. He has learned to feel that he is a man only by his physical, violent, or sexual exploits. He leaves welfare or chance to father his children and he "fathers" his car, his clothes, or his apartment. Dr. Akbar comments that, "This peculiar behavior is often characterized as a racial trait attributable to some type of moral weakness in African-American people. Such conclusions fail to identify the real origin of such traits. Such family irresponsibility does not occur among African people who have not endured the ravages of slavery."

I agree with Dr. Akbar that many of the things we are going through now are a direct result of our slavery past. We need healing and closure. The virtues of being able to protect, support, and provide for one's offspring, which is the corner-stone of true fatherhood, was not considered the mark of a Black man. In fact, the slave who sought to assert such rights for his offspring was likely to be branded as a trouble maker and either punished or killed. After several generations of such unnatural treatment, the African-American man adapted and began to avoid the role of a true father.

Conversely, the African-American woman was valued prima-rily as a breeder or sexual receptacle to show the capacity to have healthy children. Again, Goodell (1853) offers an example of a newspaper advertisement for an African woman, which dem-onstrates the desirable qualities of the slave woman.

A girl, about 20 years of age, raised in Virginia, and her two female children, one four and the other two years old. The girl is remarkably strong and healthy, never having had a day's sickness, with the exception of the smallpox, in her life. The children are fine and healthy. She is very prolific in her generating qualities and affords a rare opportunity to any person who wishes to raise a family of healthier servants for their own use.

This young slave girl's worth as a human being was reduced to particular financial value or personal pleasure she could hold for the master. As a breeder, she was to be mated with the plantation's strongest "studs," regardless of human attachment. She was also expected to be receptive to sexual exploitation of the slave master. Goodell documents this point:

> Forced concubinage of slave women with their masters and overseers, often coerced by the lash, contributed another class of facts, equally undesirable. Rape committed on a female slave is an offense not recognized by law!

> Such abuse of African-American women began to damage the natural nurturance and dignity of motherhood. Children were conceived out of convenience for an oppressor . . . not even at the level of animal lust. The child was doomed to continue in the very

conditions, abusive to their own children or over-protective of them in response to such inhumane conditions.

Today, we find many frustrated young African-American women choosing to become breeders in their search for an identity. Too many of those young mothers become abusers of those children, or turn them into delicate pimps by indulgently protecting them against a cruel world.

The massive confusion around sexual identity so often addressed in the African-American media and periodicals, has its foundation in the conditions of slavery. Men seeking to be men through physical exploits, sexual exploits, or even deviation, is predictable in a setting where natural avenues to manhood have been systematically blocked. Women will experience inevitable frustration of their natural feminine aspirations when the paths to womanhood have been blocked. The historical images which we have inherited continue to sabotage many of our efforts for true manhood (fatherhood) and womanhood (motherhood).

In nature and throughout the historical development of cultured people, the roles of man and father, woman and mother, have been inextricably bound. Only in instances of decaying culture such as ancient Greece, Rome, and modern Euro-America has this bond been broken. With its break has come family dissolution, followed closely by total societal dissolution.

Dr. Akbar comments, "Though current attitudes and conditions (such as unemployment) feed these patterns and keep them growing, the origins of the African-American family problems rest in the plague of slavery. If we understand these historical routines and patterns, then perhaps we can try to avoid continuing to play them."

And I say, "Amen," to that.

How are we ever going to come together again? We need the truth, and the truth will make us free. Truth is the motivation for this book, *Trouble In The Barnyard.* The idea of the hen-pecked husband and rooster-pecked wife comes from the realization that the years and conditions left by slavery have fostered the lack of respect and the divisions between Black men and women. With the help of God and educated men such as Dr. Akbar and others, we can come to healing and closure. The image of the Black man must change in order for the respect to come. We need a psychological healing.

I wondered for years, why we can't seem to get along. Rodney King asked that question in reference to the White and Black racial problem. We as a people do not praise and respect one another. In the sixties, Aretha Franklin recorded a song entitled "Respect." She wanted respect when she got home. It is hard to respect a man with a negative image. We need to get some answers as to why we as a people can't come together—especially the Black family. My books (*No Apology Necessary* and *Trouble In The Barnyard*) give the absolute answer.

Some say, when I am speaking on this subject, that I am pretty hard on the women; but what about the men? Well, in his speech, Willie Lynch said that the woman was most important for the controlling of the slaves. So we must give as much attention to the women as well. So if it seems in my writing, that I am spending more time dealing with the woman than the man, it is because the woman was the target in the Garden of Eden, and the woman was also the target during slavery. In the Garden of Eden, the serpent seduced Eve, and then Eve seduced Adam. Sometimes influence is stronger than authority; it certainly was in the Garden of Eden. As you read the evaluation of the Lynch speech, you'll come to understand why the woman is so important.

Lynch stated the problems of the slave masters and told them how to solve them by implementing his program. He was from the West Indies where he owned a plantation on which he experimented with some of the newest yet still the oldest methods for control of slaves. He said ancient Rome would envy them if his program were implemented.

> I have a foolproof method for controlling your black slaves. I guarantee everyone of you that if installed correctly, it will control the slaves. Any member of your family or your overseer can use it.
>
> I have outlined a number of differences among the slaves: and I take these differences and make them

bigger. I use fear, distrust, and envy for control purposes.

You know that we as a people fear, distrust, and are envious of each other, and you know that is the truth. Lynch says to take this simple little list of differences and think about them.

> On top of my list is "age," the second is "color" or "shade." There is intelligence, size, sex, size of plantations, status on plantations, attitude of the owners, whether the slaves live in the valley, on a hill, east, west, north, south, have fine hair or coarse hair, or are tall or short. Now that you have a list of differences, I shall give you an outline of action—but before that I shall assure you that distrust is stronger than trust, and envy is stronger than adulation, respect, or admiration.

> The Black slave, after receiving this indoctrination (about the differences, fear, distrust, and envy), shall carry on and will become self-refueling and self-generating for hundreds of years, maybe thousands. Don't forget, you must pitch the old Black male against the young Black male, and the young Black male against the old Black male.

I know personally cases where the older Black man despises the success of a young Black male. And some cases where the older Black males refuse to help a young Black male. They say, "Let him pull himself up by his own boot straps." Unfortunately, this even happens in the church. The old preacher is insecure and will chase a young preacher away.

You must use the dark skin against the light-skinned slaves, and the light skin against the dark-skinned slaves.

As a college freshman, a young woman ran into this light-skin/dark-skin issue at a prominent West Coast university in 1975. She had graduated from high school at the top of her class and was courted by several impressive universities from all over the country. She had the pleasant task of choosing which one of these schools she would attend and set about going down her check-list of features. One of the most important things was whether or not the college had sororities because she really wanted to pledge. Well, when she arrived at her university of choice, she wasted no time in finding out about the sorority and fraternity system. As she went from house to house during rush week, she was surprised not only to find that she was not welcomed in the sorority houses with all white members, but she was not expected to pledge a certain African-American group because of her light brown skin. This inner-race discrimination so upset her, that she decided not to pledge at all.

This young woman remembers thinking, "This is 1975. I thought we 'overcame' back with Dr. Martin Luther King, Jr. and the Civil Rights marches of the sixties."

There are families that still fall victim to this light-skin/dark-skin difference mentality. Lighter skinned children are considered cuter than their darker brothers and sisters and this is evidenced by comments and differential treatment. When you're forced to look at an issue like this, it sounds ridiculous, but the images of beauty and intelligence that are ever before us have so ingrained some assumptions in us that we are usually unaware that we hold some of these biases ourselves. Although Dr. King was referring to the Black/White racial problem, we can take a quote from the "I Have A Dream" speech to heart on the subject of the light/dark problem. We can dream, as he did, for the day when our own people "are not judged by the color of their skin, but by the content of their character."

Let's move on to another point in the Lynch letter.

You must use the female against the male, and the male against the female. You must also have all your white servants and overseers distrust all Blacks, but it is necessary that your slaves trust and depend on us. They must love, respect, and trust only us.

Did you hear what he said about the female slave versus the male slave? This is where the role reversal kicks in. You haven't heard anything yet; just keep reading. My passion for this message is because I want you to know the truth because the truth will make you free. The truth is that we are severely divided. It is my sincere hope and prayer that we begin to live before we die.

The Systematic Physical Breaking and Psychological Reversing Process

. . . Break the will to resist. Now the breaking process is the same for both the horse and the Black, only slightly varying in degrees. But as we said before, there is an art in long range economic planning. You must keep your eye and thoughts on the female and the offspring of the horse and the Black.

A brief discourse in offspring development will shed light on the key to sound economic principles. Pay little attention to the generation of original breaking but concentrate on future generations. Therefore, if you break the female mother, she will break the offspring in its early years of development, and when the offspring is old enough to work, she will deliver it up to you for her normal female productive tendencies will have been lost in the original breaking process.

For example, take the case of the wild stud horse, a female horse, and an already infant horse and compare the breaking process with two captured Black males in their natural state, a pregnant Black woman with her infant offspring. Take the stud horse, break him for limited containment. Completely break the female horse until she becomes gentle whereas you or anybody else can ride her in comfort. Breed the mare and the stud until you have the desired offspring. Then you can turn the stud to freedom until you need him again.

This is why some of our Black men can't seem to stay with one woman. He was trained on the plantation to serve as a stud. Some of the brothers think that they are so wonderful that every woman wants him, but he needs to know it's generational perpetuation; it's in his bones to hit and run and not be faithful.

Train the female horse whereby she will eat out of your hand, and she will, in turn, train the infant horse to eat out of your hand also.

When it comes to breaking the uncivilized Black, use the same process, but vary the degree and step up the pressure so as to do a complete reversal of the mind. Take the meanest and most restless Black, strip him of his clothes in front of the remaining male Blacks, the female, and the infant Black. Tar and feather him, tie each leg to a different horse faced in opposite directions, set him afire, and beat both horses to put him apart in front of the remaining Blacks. The next step is to take a bull whip and beat the remaining Black males to the point of death in front of the female and infant. Don't kill them, but put the fear of God in them, for they can be useful for future breeding.

The male image of protection has now been destroyed for the Black women and children.

Then take the female, run a series of tests on her to see if she will submit to your desires willingly. Test her in every way because she is the most important factor for good economics. If she shows any sign of resistance in submitting completely to your will, do not hesitate to use the bull whip on her to extract the last bit of bitch out of her. Take care not to kill her, for, in doing so, you spoil good economics. When in complete submission,

she will train offspring in the early years to submit to labor when they become of age.

Now you see that the success of the deception rested upon the
state of mind of the Black woman. You see her importance
within the scheme.

Understanding is the best thing. Therefore, we
shall go deeper into this area of the subject matter concerning what we produced here in this
breaking process of the female Black. We have
reversed the relationships. In her natural uncivilized state she would have a strong dependency
on the uncivilized Black male, and she would have
a limited protective tendency toward her man,
independent male offspring and would raise the
female offspring to be dependent like her. Nature
had provided for this type of balance. We reversed
nature by burning and pulling one civilized Black
apart and bull whipping the other to the point of
death—all in her presence. By her being left alone,
unprotected, with the male image destroyed, the
ordeal caused her to move from her psychological
dependent state to a frozen independent state. In
the frozen psychological state of independence she
will raise her male and female offspring in reverse
roles. For fear of the young male's life, she will

psychologically train him to be mentally weak and dependent by physically strong.

Because she has become psychologically independent, she will train her female offspring to be psychologically independent. What have you got? You've got the Black woman out front and the Black man behind and scared. This is a perfect situation for sound sleep and economics.

Before the breaking process, we had to be alertly on guard at all times. Now we can sleep soundly, for, out of frozen fear, his woman stands guard for us, he cannot get past her early infant slave molding process. He is a good tool, now ready to be tied up to the horse at a tender age."

There are an alarming number of single-parent-mother homes in which boys are being raised. Many of these women are doing a phenomenal job, however, based on Lynch's model, I think it's important to note that an unspoken message is coming through loud and clear to these boys. The message is this: Since Momma is "doing fine" without a man, Momma really doesn't need a man. Since Momma doesn't need a man, it easy to conclude that when their woman has their babies, she will be able to handle things without him. It's no big deal. Black women are strong and can handle it. They know a good woman will not abandon her babies. That's scary, isn't it?

> By the time a Black boy reaches the age of sixteen,
> he is soundly broken in and ready for a long life
> of sound and efficient work and the reproduction
> of a unit of good labor force.

This is one of the reasons the Black man is leaving his Black woman, because he is tired of being a slave. As you read on, you will see what I mean.

> Continually, through the breaking of uncivilized
> savage Blacks, by throwing the Black female savage
> into a frozen psychological state of independency,
> by killing of the protective male image, and by
> creating a submissive dependent mind of the
> Black male savage, we have created an orbiting
> cycle that turns on its own axis forever, unless a
> phenomenon occurs and reshifts the position of
> the male and female savages.

So you see, by degrading the Black man, forcing him into a submissive position, and by thrusting the Black woman into the position of control—even if merely for the sake of survival—the roles in Black relationships were reversed, thus the development of the hen-pecked husband syndrome that, unfortunately, continues in many Black families to this day. And as Lynch says himself, this "orbiting cycle" will continue to turn "on its own axis forever, unless a phenomenon occurs and reshifts the position of the male and female." It is the object of this book to be that phenomenon.

While watching the Oprah Winfrey Show, I saw a segment of her show entitled "Remembering Your Spirit." She introduced a woman pastor and I heard a voice that was so heavy I was confused. The voice sounded like a man. I said to my wife, "Are you hearing this woman's voice?" My wife is absolutely a quintessential feminine woman and she said, "That woman sounds like a man."

The title of this book, *Trouble In The Barnyard*, metaphorically addresses the issue of role reversal. On the farm, when you find a hen sounding like a rooster, you have a perverse chicken that does not realize what it is. Therefore, you have trouble in the barnyard. When that happens on the farm, that hen ends up as chicken and dumplings for dinner. The reason for getting rid of this hen who is imitating the rooster is because she confuses the other hens who are drawn to her due to her difference. She also jumps on the other hens. The rooster has lost control when she's around.

It's funny how many times parallels of human behavior can be seen in animal behavior. In this chapter, we are going to explore the issue of role reversal in terms of church leadership.

Once in Memphis at our holy convocation, a fellow minister and good friend of mine introduced me to a woman who had the title of Bishop. He wanted me to address this woman as Bishop and I said, "Are you crazy? We don't believe in women bishops."

This elder wanted a bishop to introduce this woman as a bishop to the entire convocation. I said to the elder, "I know you are crazy now. Do you ever want to be a bishop in this church? Well, if you do, you should not advocate introducing this woman to our convocation as a bishop."

I am vehemently opposed to ministers who made a vow to uphold the doctrine of our church and then refuse to do so by pushing the political agenda of women being ordained as pastors or positions of authority over men.

This same woman who was at the Memphis convocation addressed the convocation in Pennsylvania as a bishop and I was appalled. Of course, the bishop who invited her has been a proponent of that movement in the church so I shouldn't have been surprised.

Then I saw this woman at the airport upon returning home. She had overalls with masculine shoes and was walking just like a man. (I am not preaching against pants, please understand that is not my point.) If you don't want Joe to act like Josephine, then Josephine shouldn't sound and walk like Joe either. When we see Dennis Rodman dressing in a wedding dress with lipstick on his lips, a wig on his head, high heel shoes, pantyhose, and everything else that pertains to a woman, real men have a good laugh and call him Dennis the Menace, a rare bird. So, when I see the woman who called herself a bishop walking like a man with men's shoes and overalls, I would say she too is a rare bird—a hen imitating a rooster.

Another issue that I would like to address on the same lines is how some pastors are now appointing their wives as co-pastors. I say again that the doctrine of our church does not support this action. These are Ahabs controlled by Jezebels. Some pastors do this to provide security in the event of their death. The wife will then have a steady income, but is this scriptural?

Once a friend of mind made his wife the co-pastor. Co-pastor means equal in power and it also means she is over all the men as well as the women in the church. One day, while my friend was out of town, she called a fast without his permission. When he heard about it, he was angry. He has trouble in his barnyard. He called me complaining about his wife being out of control.

"I didn't tell her to call a fast," he complained.

I countered, "She didn't have to ask for your permission to call a fast because she is the co-pastor. You gave her permission by making her co-pastor."

He was shocked by my reply. As we discussed it further, I told him that there is no such thing as a co-pastor when it comes to the woman and the man. She is physically fifty percent weaker than he is. She comes from the rib of the man and not the head bone. God did not take woman out of man's feet for him to walk all over her, nor did he take her out of man's head so she could lord it over him; but He took her out of man's rib to walk along side of him as a helpmate. He took her from his left side next to his heart so man would love and cherish his wife as Christ loved the Church.

Let's get a balance from the scriptures before we make an edict.

> Wives, submit yourselves unto your own husbands,
> as it is fit in the Lord. Husbands, love your wives,
> and be not bitter against them.
> (Colossians 3:18–19)

> Let every soul be subject unto the higher powers.
> For there is no power but of God: the powers that
> be are ordained of God. (Romans 13:1)

The higher power in the home is the husband. I do not care how short he is, he is still the higher power. In the courtroom, it's the judge; on the job, it's the boss; in the school, it's the principal and the teachers; and in the church, the higher power is the pastor.

When my friend made his wife the co-pastor, he usurped the authority of God. He took the power God gave him and gave it to his wife. To usurp means to seize and hold a position, function, or prerogative rightly belonging to another, so that was a power that was not his to give.

> But I suffer not a woman to teach, nor to usurp
> authority over the man, but to be in silence. For
> Adam was first formed, then Eve. And Adam was
> not deceived, but the woman being deceived was
> in the transgression. (1 Timothy 2:12–14)

Also, I believe it is necessary at this point for me to say that Paul is not saying women must be quiet in worship and while prophesying. Paul is talking about usurping authority over a man. He referred to the Garden of Eden to demonstrate that there has always been a divine order in the male/female relationship. Remember again in the book of Esther about King Ahasuerus's decree that husbands small and great were to be given honor in their homes and that each man was to rule in his own house.

Recently this issue of ordaining women pastors was on the floor of the General Assembly and several persons addressed it. However, one lady, Evangelist Drusslia Carter (no relation to me) stood and made a profound plea that the church should not compromise or change the doctrine or destroy the foundational legacy of doctrinal balance left to us by our saintly father, Bishop Charles H. Mason.

I say, "Amen," to that.

You may ask, "What harm could it be to have a woman pastor or co-pastor?"

Again, let's look to scripture for our answers. In the letter to Thyatira found in Revelation 21:18–29, we read of "the woman

Jezebel, who calleth herself a prophetess," and led some members of the Christian church to commit spiritual fornication. This may be a symbolic name, given because of a resemblance between her and the idolatrous wife of Ahab. Thyatira was the papal church and a prosperous trading center. It was famous for the manufacture of purple dyes and for its clothing industries. The church at Thyatira was characterized by externalism. It was a great church organization and did a lot of socializing. The last part of verse 19 says there were more works than there was faith.

Also, the church at Thyatira was sapped by "Jezebelianism." Jezebel was the wife of King Ahab. She was a wicked and obstinate woman. She tried to combine Israel's worship of the true God with the worship of the idol Baal. In John's day, there was likely a woman leader in the church of Thyatira who was somewhat like the Old Testament Jezebel. The Lord says in verse 20, "I have a few things against thee," and in verse 23 says, "that those who follow her ways will meet death." The people at Thyatira were given over to idolatry. Notice in verse 24, there was a group within the church at Thyatira who continued in the faith and had not been deceived by Jezebel. The Lord tells the faithful ones to "hold fast til I come." This indicates that it is possible to be loyal to the cause of Christ even in the midst of apostasy.

The church at Thyatira pictures a period in Church history known as the Middle Ages. This was the time when the Roman church with all its idolatry, (e.g. statues, holy water, worship of Mary, etc.) came into power. In fact, the word *thyatira* means "a continual sacrifice," and thus pictures the long period of history from 500 A.D. to 1500 A.D. when Roman Catholicism had control over nearly all of Christendom.

Although this church was commended for it good works, love, service, faithfulness and patience, it still received a condemnation—"notwithstanding I have a few things against thee" (Rev. 2:20). God's main objection with this church centered on the fact that they were allowing the ministry of a false prophetess aptly named Jezebel. Her sin was teaching men, which is forbidden (see 1 Tim. 2:12–14). She was also teaching immorality and idolatry and was totally unrepentant. Her followers will go through the great tribulation and become the false churches in Revelation 17. Her children (followers) will suffer the second death at the White Throne of Judgment (Rev. 20:11–15). She would serve as an example to other churches concerning the wrath of God. (See also Acts 5:11–13; 1 Tim. 5:22)

Jesus counsels the church by saying, "But unto you I say, and unto the rest of Thyatira as many as have not this doctrine, and which have not known the depths of Satan, as they speak; I will put upon you none other burden. But that which ye have already hold fast till I come" (Rev. 2:24) Sometimes the Church becomes so political that it compromises the truth and lets the things that are not God's will continue for the sake of peace. But the word of God speaks to this tendency:

Therefore, brethren, stand fast, and hold the
traditions which ye have been taught, whether
by word or our epistle. Comfort your hearts, and
stablish you in every good word and work.
(2 Thessalonians 2:15, 17)

The Church must stand on the principles of God without
being politically correct. So, what does the Word of God teach
about women in the Church and more specifically, women in the
ministry? Let's begin with 1 Timothy 2:12–14:

But I suffer not a woman to teach, nor to usurp
authority over the man, but to be in silence. For
Adam was first formed, then Eve. And Adam was
not deceived, but the woman being deceived was
in the transgression.

In Greek, the word *authority* means to have power over. Paul
is saying here that women should not dictate to men, but exer-
cise their rights to teach, prophesy, and pray and do other things
under the authority of men.

But every woman that prayeth or prophesieth with
her head uncovered dishonoureth her head: for
that is even all one as if she were shaven.
(1 Corinthians 11:5)

From this verse, we see that women are permitted to speak in prayer and in prophecy. If they couldn't speak at all, then how would they even worship? The scripture says, "Let everything that hath breath praise the Lord" (Psalm 150:6). So, the difficulty does not rest with women who speak or pray in the church. The difficulty is with female *leadership* in the church, usurping authority over men, such as women being pastors, bishops, or holding any office that puts her directly over men. In 1 Corinthians 14:34, women are not to be lawless or cause confusion in the church business meetings. It was the custom then for men to speak up in public assemblies, ask questions and even interrupt the speaker whey they didn't understand, but this liberty was not granted to women.

> But I would have you know, that the head of every man is Christ; and the head of the woman is the man; and the head of Christ is God.
> (1 Corinthians 11:3)

> Let your women keep silence in the churches: for it is not permitted unto them to speak; but they are commanded to be under obedience, as also saith the law. And if they will learn any thing, let them ask their husbands at home: for it is a shame for women to speak in the church.
> (1 Corinthians 14:34–35)

Now this is the same Paul to whom God gave the doctrine of *grace* for which we all thank the Lord. So Paul is not being legalistic, he's stating a rule—not a Mosaic law, but a *principle*. A principle is a force that cannot be stopped, like that of gravity.

> Likewise, ye husbands, dwell with them according to knowledge, giving honour unto the wife, as unto the weaker vessel, and as being heirs together of the grace of life; that your prayers be not hindered. (1 Peter 3:7)

Women are the weaker vessel. Therefore, can the weaker lead the stronger? I don't think so. When things are out of order, God judges. Part of the reason for God's judgment at one time on Jerusalem and Judah was because they allowed women to rule (See Is. 3:12). The leading women caused the people to go astray.

> The LORD standeth up to plead, and standeth to judge the people. The LORD will enter into judgment with the ancients of his people, and the princes thereof: for ye have eaten up the vineyard; the spoil of the poor is in your houses. What mean ye that ye beat my people to pieces, and grind the faces of the poor? saith the Lord GOD of hosts. Moreover the LORD saith, Because the *daughters of Zion* are haughty, and walk with

> stretched forth necks and wanton eyes, walking
> and mincing as they go, and making a tinkling
> with their feet: therefore the LORD will smite
> with a scab the crown of the head of the *daugh-
> ters of Zion,* and the LORD will discover their
> secret parts. (Isaiah 3:13–17, emphasis mine)

Before God judged them, they were haughty with their noses in the air. They had wanton eyes and they wore ornaments about their feet and chains around their ankles. They had veils of shimmering gauze, they wore head bands, nose jewels, and earrings. They sported party clothes and they wore ornate combs and carried purses. When God judged them, the perfumes were exchanged for a stench, the waistband for a rough cord of poverty, and the abundance of flowing hair by repulsive baldness.

The passage concludes by adding that these women's husbands would fail in the war, her gates would lament and mourn, and she would end up just sitting on the ground. (Isaiah 3:25–26)

How far removed all this was from Peter's description of real beauty and adornment. What a contrast between Isaiah 3: 24–26 and 1 Peter 3:1–4.

> Likewise, ye wives, be in subjection to your own
> husbands; that, if any obey not the word, they also
> may without the word be won by the conversa-
> tion of the wives; While they behold your chaste

conversation coupled with fear. Whose adorning let it not be that outward adorning of plaiting the hair, and of wearing of gold, or of putting on of apparel; But let it be the hidden man of the heart, in that which is not corruptible, even the ornament of a meek and quiet spirit, which is in the sight of God of great price. (1 Peter 3:1–4)

And it shall come to pass, that instead of sweet smell there shall be stink; and instead of a girdle a rent; and instead of well set hair baldness; and instead of a stomacher a girding of sackcloth; and burning instead of beauty. Thy men shall fall by the sword, and thy mighty in the war. And her gates shall lament and mourn; and she being desolate shall sit upon the ground. (Isaiah 3:24–26)

Let's take a deeper look at Isaiah 3:12 in the Pulpit Commentary:[8]

As for my people. Return is now made to sins of the dwellers in Jerusalem, and the first thing noted is that the people suffer from the childishness and effeminacy of their rulers.

The rulers were womanly, (i.e. weak, wavering, timid, impulsive, passionate, and are therefore called actual women). There is no illusion to female sovereigns. "They which lead thee cause thee to err;" or "they which guide you lead you astray."

We need strong leaders who will lead with strength and not with weakness.

Chapter Three

Bishop Jezebel

On the cover of a well-known Christian magazine, I saw the picture of a woman bishop, and I knew it was wrong. Yet when I talked to one of our general board members about this issue he said he didn't care one way or the other. He said that it didn't make any difference. He was muddling, and being politically correct. I used to think that way until, after much study on the subject, I discovered the truth.

While writing this book, the grand old Church of God in Christ seems to be divided over the issue of women wanting to be ordained as pastors of churches and perhaps even as bishops. I recently heard of one female pastor who stated, "I *will* be the first woman bishop in the Church of God in Christ."

But not everyone agrees. One year, the presiding bishop in his annual address said, "We are going to loose the women and give them more freedom to work in the ministry."

"Oh!" the women shouted for joy with great expectation. Then, however, the Bishop told the story of what happened to a hen who crowed like a rooster. There was a holy hush in the church! This is an issue that won't go away, so let's explore this issue a little further.

In the previous chapter, I introduced you to Willie Lynch and what he taught slave owners. Willie reversed the role of male and female, making the woman the leader and the man the follower. According to Webster's New World Dictionary,[9] *to follow* is also "to be a disciple, one who follows another's teaching; to use as a model; imitate, to obey." At times, the Church seems to be muddling on the issue of women in the ministry. We need a clear answer.

Because of Willie Lynch's speech and the current imbalance that's apparent in this society, I must write in the spirit of Elijah and he shall correct all things. (See Matthew 17:11). I facetiously called Jezebel "Bishop Jezebel" only to be scandalous, to offend some and to entertain others. Whenever you see the spirit of Jezebel, the spirit of Elijah is also around. This spirit of Elijah will always fight the spirit of Jezebel. If Jezebel wins, the soul of the nation is lost. But if Elijah wins, the soul of the nation will be saved (See Revelation 2:18–26).

While I was watching the C-SPAN public affairs network one night, I saw Minister Louis Farrakhan giving a speech. I noticed there weren't any women on the platform with the men. Beautiful African-American women were supporting the speech of Farrakhan and the men that were on the platform. They didn't seem to mind that they weren't on the platform with the men.

Later, as I was speaking with the men in my favorite barber shop, they told me that they liked Farrakhan and the Islamic teaching because they celebrated and respected male leadership. And these men also pointed out the fact that the Christian church does not adhere to that same platform. This is one of the reasons we must, as a Church, address this issue with Biblical correction. I am not anti-women in ministry, I am against women going against male authority.

Aliens Among Us

There are three principalities we are fighting: the Babylonian Spirit; the Jezebelian Spirit; and the Spirit of the Antichrist. The Babylonian Spirit is the spirit of compromise; the Jezebelian Spirit is the spirit of anti-male authority; and the Antichrist Spirit is the spirit that is against *the* things of the Christ which is Jesus. Pastor Dick Bernal wrote a book entitled, *When Lucifer and Jezebel Join Your Church.*[10] He says:

The Jezebel Spirit works through women or effeminate men. The Lucifer spirit works primarily through men. Both are very religious, gifted, powerful, influential, and strong-willed. Lucifer means "light bearer or star." Jezebel means "where is Baal?" Both usurped authority. Both were unhappy in subordinate roles. Both were wily, scheming, opposing and deceptive. These spirits are attached to strong, prophetic, charismatic, faith churches. These spirits will work through some of the nicest people you've ever met—gifted, loyal, giving, praying, volunteering people who look like an answer to prayer, and they may be at first. But because of a character flaw, a wound that never healed, or some other dysfunctional trait that was underground for a season, these nice people are easy prey for these spirits.

Here are some characteristics of the Lucifer and Jezebel Spirits:

The Lucifer & Jezebel Spirit

1. Looks for authority without much responsibility,

2. Always warns you about other leaders,

3. Gives special gifts to the pastor and spouse,

4. Asks you to bend the rules for him or her every now and then,

5. Starts to have his or her own following,

6. Doesn't show up on Sunday if some big shot is preaching at another church,

7. Gives irregularly—inconsistently,

8. Always has a "word" for you or a letter,

9. Needs constant attention,

10. Wants desperately to be an elder or pastor.

The system of the nations has invaded the house of God, and we know who it is who is behind it all, Satan. Before he fell, Lucifer was in heaven working in close proximity to God. As a matter of fact, he was head of the choir and led praise and worship. But pride infiltrated his heart and he refused to remain what God had made him. He exalted himself.

> How art thou fallen from heaven, O Lucifer, son of the morning! how art thou cut down to the ground, which didst weaken the nations! For thou hast said in thine heart, I will ascend into heaven, I will exalt my throne above the stars of God: I will sit also upon the mount of the congregation, in the sides of the north: I will ascend above the

heights of the clouds; I will be like the most High. (Isaiah 14:12–14)

And there was war in heaven: Michael and his angels fought against the dragon; and the dragon fought and his angels, and prevailed not; neither was their place found any more in heaven. And the great dragon was cast out, that old serpent, called the Devil, and Satan, which deceiveth the whole world: he was cast out into the earth, and his angels were cast out with him. (Revelation 12:7–9)

After being thrown out of Heaven, Satan wasn't extremely happy and he is still quite upset today. He has been trying to get back at God ever since. He messed up God's highest creation in the Garden of Eden when he successfully tempted Adam and Eve. Then, after being warned that the seed of the woman would crush his head, Satan went about killing all Godly men, prophets, and kings, desperately trying to wipe out this head-crusher. He thought he had it made when he killed Jesus, but of course, God had an answer for that with the resurrection. After this, the apostles went about planting churches all over the globe, so the Gospel message continues to be propagated.

Therefore, we as the Church are in spiritual warfare whether we know it or not, and whether we like it or not. Satan entered Ananias and Sapphira causing them to sin (Acts 5:3) and Paul warns us in Romans 6:16 saying, "Know ye not, that to whom ye yield yourselves servants to obey, his servants ye are to whom ye obey; whether of sin unto death, or of obedience unto righteousness?" Also remember 2 Corinthians 11:14 which reminds us, "And no marvel; for Satan himself is transformed into an angel of light."

I believe that some people are controlled by principalities and spirits as I mentioned previously. Some may ask, "How can a child of God be controlled by demons or principalities?" Roman 6:16 says, "Know ye not, that to whom ye yield yourselves servants to obey, his servants ye are to whom ye obey; whether of sin unto death, or of obedience unto righteousness?" When you fail to yield yourself to God according to his Word, you open yourself to demonic influence and become a servant of that influence. I am sure many will agree that sometimes we see Christians who seem be totally out of character without corresponding action to the Word of God. That person, at that particular time, is being a servant to demonic influence and thus becomes an alien.

We must be aware that we Christians are in spiritual warfare, for Ephesians 6:11-12 says: "Put on the whole armor of God, that ye may be able to stand against the wiles of the devil. For we wrestle not against flesh and blood, but against principalities, against powers, against the rulers of the darkness of this world, against spiritual wickedness in high places."

In their book *Pigs In The Parlor*,[11] A. Frank & Ida Mae Hammond state that "Demons are evil personalities. They are spirit beings. They are the enemies of God and man. Their objectives in human beings are to tempt, deceive, accuse, condemn, pressure, defile, resist, oppose, control, steal, afflict, kill and destroy."

Demons enter through "open doors." They have to be given an opportunity. There must be an opening. In other words, one does not pick up a demon by walking down the street and accidentally bumping into one that is looking for a home.

The organization of Satan's kingdom enables him to attack each of us personally. There is not a person on the face of the earth who escapes his notice. He devises a plan to ruin and destroy each one. It is a sobering realization that you and I are definite targets of Satan's wiles. But how does he gain entrance? SIN.

The door for demons to enter may be opened through sins of omission and commission. In the fifth chapter of Acts we read of a couple named Ananias and Sapphira. They sold their property so they could give the full proceeds for the benefit of the church. But they became covetous and decided to keep part for themselves. In order to cover up their act they perpetrated a lie. But Peter received a supernatural word of knowledge as to what they had done. Peter asked Ananias why he had opened himself to the Devil.

But Peter said, "Ananias, why hath Satan filled thine heart to lie to the Holy Ghost, and to keep back part of the price of the land?" (Acts 5:3).

Because of their sin, Ananias and Sapphira opened themselves to be filled with spirits of covetousness and deceit. The same thing can happen to anyone who sins willfully.

In the fifth chapter of Galatians we find a list of seventeen "works of the flesh." They include the sins of adultery, fornication, witchcraft, hatred, wrath, strife, envying, murders and drunkenness. Through my experiences in deliverance I have encountered demons that responded to each of these designations. What, then, is the relationship between the works of the flesh and the works of demons? When a man yields to temptation he sins in the flesh. Through such sin the door is opened for the invasion of the enemy. Then he has a compounded problem; the flesh *and* the devil. The solution is two-fold: crucify the flesh and cast out the demons.

A classic example of the door being opened by the sin of omission is the failure to forgive. In the case of the unjust steward (Matt. 18) he was turned over to the "tormentors" because he was unwilling to forgive his fellow servant after he himself had been forgiven by his master. God warns us that all who have experienced His forgiveness and refuse to forgive others will be turned over to the tormentors. What clearer designation of demon spirits can we find than "tormentors?" Unforgiveness opens the door to the torment of resentment, hatred, and related spirits.

I believe that the church is under the attack of the devil to destroy the structure and order of God. The Anti-Christ spirit hates God order. "Anti" means against—he opposes everything that God is for. If God says "left" the devil will say "right." He attacks Christians and weakens them so they become weak morally, but that is not the worst part. His real goal is to destroy the doctrine of the Church which provides scriptural structure.

I like what Win Worley said in his book *Christians Can and Do Have Demons.*[12] He said Paul reproves the Corinthian Christians for receiving another spirit than the Spirit they had previously received (2 Corinthians 11:4). This is a case in which the language of the King James translation does not fully convey the force of the original.

The Phillips translation says: "For apparently you cheerfully accept a man who comes to you preaching a different Jesus than the one we told you about, and you readily receive a spirit and a gospel quite different from the one you originally accepted." Or, as the Living Bible puts it, "You swallow it all."

Paul inquired, in Galatians 3:1, about who had bewitched the believers to draw them away from the truth. "Bewitched" carries the overtones of the use of witchcraft and the casting of spells. The effects upon them were not just the effects of wrong mental impressions conveyed by false teachers. It involved evil spirits imposing false doctrine through false teachers. These references emphatically suggest that believers do not enjoy an easy exemption from the activities of demons. Rather, they are particularly targeted by them for attack.

Robert Peterson makes an interesting comment: "It appears that the full force of deceiving spirits is directed against the spiritual believer in doctrinal, rather than worldly, matters, although the latter may be used after the believer has been ensnared by the more subtle means. In 1 Timothy 4:1,2 the apostle Paul gives a full account of how wicked spirits attack the spiritual believer and by deception beguile him away from the faith through the use of false prophets."

I perceive that the church world is under attack doctrinally, to get us off track concerning God's order according to His word from which we get our doctrine. 2 Timothy 3:16, "All scripture is given by inspiration of God, and is profitable for doctrine, for reproof, for correction, for instruction in righteousness." Doctrine is something that is taught; a principle or body of principles presented for acceptance or belief, or as by religion.

We should be strong and mature in our doctrinal stand. We should not be a Toys-R-Us Church who does not want to grow up. Ephesians 4:14 says, "That we henceforth be no more children, tossed to and fro, and carried about with every wind of doctrine, by the sleight of men, and cunning craftiness, whereby they lie in wait to deceive."

At this time in the church, we have leaders who seem to be more political than scriptural. I talked to one candidate for the presiding bishop concerning this matter of ordaining women to be pastors, as that is not the doctrine of our church. Some leaders are afraid to deal with this issue because of its political incorrectness, but I will continue to move in the spirit of Elijah to correct all things.

As a man of God, I chose to be a good minister as it is said in 1 Timothy 4:1-2, 6, "Now the Spirit speaketh expressly, that in the latter times some shall depart from the faith, giving heed to seducing spirits, and doctrines of devils; Speaking lies in hypocrisy; having their conscience seared with a hot iron; If thou put the brethren in remembrance of these things, thou shalt be a good minister of Jesus Christ, nourished up in the words of faith and of good doctrine, whereunto thou has attained."

It takes courage and strong convictions to stand for what you believe to be the right doctrine, but now we have leaders who seem to not believe the doctrine of our church concerning women being ordained as pastors. They chose rather to be political rather than scriptural.

The Church of God in Christ, the church that I love, does not ordain women to be pastors to usurp authority over men. In 1 Corinthians 11:1, Paul said, "Be ye followers of me, even as I also am of Christ. Now I praise you, brethren, that ye remember me in all things, and keep the ordinances, as I delivered them to you. But I would have you know, that the head of every man is Christ: and the head of the woman is the man; and the head of Christ is God."

I am a follower of Paul and a follower of Christ. For Christ called Paul to be Apostle and gave him the revelation of Church order and doctrine. I recognize Paul as the demons also recognize Paul as shown with the sons of Sceva, Act 19:14,15; "And there were seven sons of one Sceva, a Jew, and chief of the priests, which did so. And the evil spirit answered and said, *Jesus I know and Paul I know; but who are ye?"*

I would like to say at this time when it comes down to the doctrine of the church; Jesus, I know, Paul I know, and Bishop Mason I know, but the rest of the leaders who seem to be comprising, political and muddling, I do not know. Therefore, there is no real need for the church manual, which contains the doctrine of the church. If we are not going to abide by it, we need to change it, but until we change it, we need to obey it. When pastors make their wives co-pastors, that is in violation of doctrine of our church and we should deal with it, to get past the impasse and bring closure to this matter.

Let's take another look at more characteristics of Jezebel:

The Jezebel Spirit

1. Is very religious,

2. Is clever,

3. Loves power and authority,

4. Goes after leadership,

5. Tries to pull people away from their true covering, the pastor and the church,

6. Loves titles (i.e. Prophetess, Elder, etc.),

7. Uses flattery, sex, witchcraft, lies, etc. to gain control,

8. Uses intimidation by means of other people, letters, telephone,

9. Quick to judge and advise,

10. Loves prophetic, faith, and charismatic circles,

11. Very patronizing,

12. Has a cultic following and claims to be discipling them,

13. Her Christian-ese is impeccable,

14. Very inquisitive about the pastor's personal life (spouse, family) and about church business,

15. Hot-tempered,

16. Into preserving her little kingdom at all costs,

17. Controls her following with dictatorial tactics.

After reading about Lucifer and Jezebel, I am very certain that pastors and anyone who has been involved with church for any significant amount of time can relate to what I am saying. A pastor friend of mine called one day and said, "Carter, I have a young lady evangelist at my church. Man, she is doing a fantastic job. The people just love her. She can get those people to do things that I can't get them to do. But, there is something about her that I just can't put my finger on. I don't really understand how she has so much power over these people."

He went on to say that whatever she asked the people to give in the offering, they would give it. Oh boy, she seemed to be an answer to prayer. He even sat the other ministers down and allowed her to raise the Sunday morning offerings. Every Monday, he would call me excited about this wonderful young "lady evangelist." He would wash my face with this wonderful news of a great time in the service and how the offerings were growing because of this wonderful young lady. He knew my feelings about headship and wanted me to change my views about men being in charge of leadership in the church, and women working alongside to help as Paul stated in Scripture.

This went on for a while. I told him that one day her true spirit would come to light. It finally happened. On this particular Sunday, she was up conducting the offering service and it happened. When the deacons weren't moving fast enough for her, she said, "You are all moving like a bunch of knuckle heads." That was the Jezebel spirit coming out. She was out of order and something had to be done. When the hen acts like a rooster, you have trouble in the barnyard.

The wives of the deacons went to the pastor and said they don't talk to their husbands in that way, and they certainly weren't going to let another woman talk to their husbands that way. This friend of mine had to get that hen out of the barnyard.

Another example happened when a prophetess went to a town near Orlando, Florida. She had people coming to church at

3:00 am for service. They brought jewelry of all kinds, even a lawnmower. She could get people to do what even the pastor couldn't get them to do.

Sometimes this spirit is operating through people and they don't know it. This same woman in Florida loves to appear very humble and nobody is quite as holy as she purports herself to be. Of course, her "Christian-eze" is impeccable. On one occasion, she took a lady's Bible, looked in it and noticed it wasn't marked up well enough for her, so she told the lady, "You don't read your Bible enough." I don't know anyone who reads his or her Bible enough, including this prophetess I'm talking about.

Another thing I noticed about this lady was that she gives very little Word, but uses mystical expressions and speaks in a loud voice to keep the attention of her audience. Mysticism creeps into the vocabulary and behavior of women with the Jezebel Spirit. In their book entitled *Integrity* by Ted W. Engstrom and Robert Larson,[13] they explain more about mysticism:

> Mysticism is the perennial temptation to turn away from the pursuit of pleasure and power in search of union with the Eternal. The penetration of Eastern religions into the industrial West has presented a new alternative for tens of thousands of people. Mysticism is usually a world-denying type of philosophy, but some neomystics stress immersion in the world, finding God in the depths of human existence.

Whereas secular humanism celebrates the fulfillment of the self, mysticism emphasizes the loss of
the self in the collective unconscious, the cosmic
process, or the undifferentiated unity. Mysticism is
especially prevalent among those in our churches
and theological schools who are intent on recover-
ing spirituality. It is also found among radical femi-
nists, particularly those who are trying to reinstate
the nature religion of witchcraft.

Matthew Henry's commentary speaks about Jezebel in
Revelation 2 and suggests that there was a person or persons
who were seducers and these wicked seducers are compared
to Jezebel and called her by name. The sin of these seducers
was that they attempted to draw the servants of God into
fornication and to offer sacrifices to idols. They called themselves prophets and so would claim superior authority in
regards to the ministers of the church. These seducers called
their doctrines "profound mysteries" and they would amuse
the people, endeavoring to persuade them that they had a
deeper insight than the ministers had attained. Christ called
these seducers the "depths of Satan." They used satanic
delusions and devices and diabolical mysteries. There is a
mystery of iniquity as well as the mystery of Godliness. It is
dangerous to receive the mysteries of Satan. Yet, how tender
Christ is to his faithful servants:

But unto you I say, and unto the rest in Thyatira, as many as have not this doctrine, and which have not known the depths of Satan, as they speak; I will put upon you none other burden. But that which ye have already hold fast till I come. (Revelation 2:24–25)

Christ says he will not overburden your faith with any new mysteries, nor your conscience with any new laws. He only requires your attention to what you have received. Hold what you have until He comes and He desires no more.

It's bad when a person comes to town and the pastor has no control because of this mystical wonder. Once the Jezebel hen grasps the attention of the other hens, the rooster can't do anything in the barnyard. Anytime you can't have service because someone else has control over the people, the pastor (just like the rooster) is no longer the leader, Jezebel is. Don't forget, she fed the prophets of Baal at her table every day.

Late one night, I got a phone call from a young man who is a minister. He told me a story I will never forget. He arrived home early one evening only to find his wife with another man in his bedroom in a compromising position. In shock, he ran out of the door, surprised and hurt by all that he had witnessed. Of course, the other man was afraid and ran away. After the young minister had calmed down, he and his wife sat down to discuss the matter. His wife explained that she didn't know what came over her to do such a thing, but she wouldn't do it again. I almost dropped the phone when I heard this story! He forgave her and they moved out of the area, hoping that would solve the problem. Unfortunately, it only got worse. This wife started seeing another man *and* a woman. At the same time, she was leading praise and worship in the church.

Knowing her problem, the young minister confronted her and told her that she needed help. She cried, but never got delivered. The reason I'm relating this story to you now is because of the most recent news I've heard about this woman. She is now ordained as a prophetess-evangelist in the ministry. My minister friend has divorced this woman and is married to a wife who is not an 'alien'. Beware, Jezebel is on the loose, and she *is* an alien!

COGIC Doctrine

The doctrine of the Church of God in Christ is very clear regarding women in ministry.

> The Church of God in Christ recognizes that there are thousands of talented, Spirit-filled, dedicated, and well-informed devout women capable of conducting affairs of a church, both administratively and spiritually. Such women were mentioned in the New Testament, Romans 16:1–2, "I commend unto you Phebe our sister, which is a servant of the church which is at Cenchrea: That ye receive her in the Lord, as becometh saints, and that ye

assist her in whatsoever business she hath need of you: for she hath been a succourer of many, and of myself also." Romans 16:3 "Greet Priscilla and Aquila my helpers in Christ Jesus." Aquila and Priscilla had a church in their home. Acts 18:24–28, Priscilla is equally gifted with her husband as an expounder of "the way of God" and instructor of Apollos. Acts 9:36 "Now there was at Joppa a certain disciple named Tabitha, which by interpretation is called Dorcas: this woman was full of good works and almsdeeds which she did." Acts 16:14, Lydia of Thyatira, a seller of purple, whose hospitality made a home for Paul and a meeting place for the infant church.

It is evident in the New Testament and in the writings of the Apostolic Fathers that women, through the agency of two ecclesiastical orders were assigned official duties in the conduct and ministrations of the early church. Their existence as a distinct order is indicated in I Timothy 5:9–10 where Paul directs Timothy as to the conditions of their enrollment. No widow should be enrolled under 60 years of age having been the wife of one man. She must be "well reported of good works," "a mother having brought up children," "hospitable," having "used hospitality to strangers,"

Christ-like in loving service, having "washed the saints' feet."

Other special duties mentioned by the Church Fathers included prayer and fasting, visiting the sick, instruction of women, preparing them for baptism, assisting in the administration of this ordinance, and taking the communion.

Many of the duties of the widows were transferred to the deaconesses by the Third Century, an order which in recent history has been restored to its original importance and effectiveness.

The Church of God in Christ recognizes the scriptural importance of women in the Christian Ministry, (Matthew 28:1; Mark 16:1; Luke 24:1; John 20:1), the first at the tomb on the morning of Christ's resurrection; the first to whom the Lord appeared (Matthew 28:9; Mark 16:9; John 20:14), the first to announce the fact of the resurrection to the chosen disciples (Luke 29:9, 10:22), and etc., but nowhere can we find a mandate to ordain women to be an Elder, Bishop, or Pastor. Women may teach the gospel to others (Phil. 4:3; Titus 2:3–5; Joel 2:28), have charge of a church in absence of its pastor, if the pastor so wishes, (Romans 16:1–5) without adopting the title of Elder, Reverend, Bishop, or Pastor. Paul styled the women who labored with him as servants or helpers, not Elders, Bishops, or Pastors. Therefore the Church of God in Christ cannot accept the following scriptures as a mandate to ordain women preachers—Joel 2:28; Galatians 3:28–29; Matthew 28:9–11. The qualifications for Elder, Bishop, or Pastor are found in 1 Timothy 3:2–7 and Titus 1:7–9. We exhort all to take heed.

Church of God in Christ official manual[14]

I would like to also say that the Catholic Church does not ordain women to be priests, but they do make them missionaries. Who could ever forget Mother Teresa? She left a mark on the earth by being a humble servant in Calcutta by working with the poor. This quintessential missionary gave up her life, and found life. She ran from fame, but fame ran her down.

Unlike Jesus who ran from the crowd and got the crowd, we are running after the crowd and never reaching the crowd. Therefore, the question of ministry should not be a question of position. Mother Teresa never tried to be a priest or the pope, but became just as famous as the pope.

We have some "missionaries" driving Mercedes, living in million-dollar homes, staying in the finest hotels, living large with designer clothes and ordering room service. And if they're not treated like movie stars, they have the nerve to say they're suffering for Jesus. The missionary evangelists in our country are the best paid in the world. If you were to catch some of them while they were asleep and put them on a boat going to a foreign field, they would jump off when they woke up and swim back to shore if it were possible. How unlike Mother Teresa, who was concerned about humanity rather than fame and fortune.

You don't have to be a bishop, pastor, or elder to be used by God. You only have to be a willing servant. I shall never forget our own late Mother Elsie Shaw, a real woman of God and I might add, a very feminine and refined lady. I would say she was decked down with femininity and dripping with grace. She was a sophisticated lady. I can picture her now standing in Memphis, praying as she prophesied about the fires in Los Angeles, and about the coldest winters in my life when the antifreeze was frozen in cars in some parts of the country. She was a woman who had a rhema word rather than the logos. The average Christian can recite the logos but it takes a consecrated, dedicated person of God to deal with the rhema. Sister Shaw didn't need a title, she had God.

The Church of God in Christ is experiencing outside interference from those who want to substitute the doctrine of "headship" for the doctrine of "sameship." Have you ever heard the phrase, "If it's not broken, don't fix it?" We should leave things as they are and make it on what "is." It didn't work when the children of Israel wanted to change their manna recipe (Numbers 11:4–9), and it's not going to work for us to try to change

God's leadership recipe. Some are trying to change everything, following others on this subject. We have some leaders who are muddling, being political and not scriptural. We need to stop muddling and have courage of our convictions.

One year Pope John Paul II visited Philadelphia. At one of the conferences during his visit, a nun went up to the microphone and asked him about ordaining women into the priesthood. The pope answered by saying, "Next person, please." He didn't even dignify the question with an answer because he knew what he believed and didn't muddle.

Jude verse 3 states, " . . . earnestly contend for the faith which was once delivered unto the saints." It is impossible to always be positive while contending the truth. H. A. Ironside, a long-time pastor of Moody Memorial Church in Chicago declared, "The faith means the whole body of revealed truth, and to contend for all of God's truth necessitates some negative teaching . . . Any error, or any truth-and-error mixture calls for definite exposure and repudiation. To condone such is to be unfaithful to God and His word, and treacherous to imperiled souls for whom Christ died."

Dave Wilkerson, a pastor, best-selling author and founder of Teen Challenge has said, "There is an evil wind . . . blowing into God's house, deceiving multitudes of God's chosen people."

Deborah, YES. Jezebel, NO.

So what do we do about gifted women of God who pray, prophesy, speak, and counsel in church and at retreats and conferences all over the country? There is no denying that these women are used of God to bless His people. Many of these female "prophets" are learned in the Word of God and their messages are Biblically sound. I contend that the difference between these holy women and their sisters who want the title of pastor, elder, or bishop, is the same as the difference that exists between Deborah and Jezebel.

Jezebel is against male authority and unable to cohabitate with anyone unless she's in control. But Deborah, a judge in Israel, was humble and was used of God to prophesy to Israel concerning the victory over Sisera (Judges 4:4). When Barak was told to go to battle, he said to Deborah, "If thou wilt go with me, then I will go: but if thou wilt not go with me, then I will not go." Here is one man who admitted he needed the help of a woman. The Septuagint adds, "If the Lord would prosper the angel with me," meaning that he depended upon her contact with God to tell him when to attack.

Also, Judges 5:12–13 says, "Awake, awake, Deborah: awake, awake, utter a song: Arise, Barak, and lead thy captivity captive, thou son of Abinoam. Then he made him that remaineth have dominion over the nobles among the people: the LORD made me have dominion over the mighty." Deborah seems to go back in thought to the moment when she received the divine call to her mission of deliverance.

In the battle of life, a great variety of service is required for final success. Deborah could not lead the army, but she could inspire it. Barak couldn't prophesy, but he could fight. Thus,

Barak cannot secure victory without Deborah. They needed each other to get the job done. And after all, isn't this the way the male/female relationship was originally designed to work?

There is work for both the seer and the warrior. Deborah, the prophetess, is gifted with the wisdom and the enthusiasm of direct inspiration and thus becomes the inspirer of Barak and his troops. Barak feels that if Deborah goes along with him, God's counsel and encouragement will be given. Therefore, Deborah is symbolically used like the Holy Spirit, the paraclete, the one who works alongside to help.

God also uses instruments of weakness to demonstrate his power as stated in I Corinthians 1:27 so that no flesh should glory in His presence (I Corinthians 1:29). The following eight weak things of Judges were used by God to confound the mighty:

1. the left hand (3:21),

2. an ox-goad (3:31),

3. a nail (4:21),

4. a piece of millstone (9:53),

5. a pitcher (7:20),

6. a trumpet (7:20),

7. a jawbone of an ass (15:16),

8. a woman (4:4, 21; 9:53).

There is no need for the women in the Church to take on titles like bishop, elder, and pastor in order to be greatly used by God. Perhaps more is being left undone because women have moved out of their place of support for the men of God, thus leaving the men handicapped in regard to their potential to do the work of the Lord to the fullest.

Chapter Four

Vashti Doesn't Live Here Anymore

ook at homes today. There's very little order in many of them, and this lack of authority spills over into society and the Church. The Church should be giving direction in this matter, spilling over into the home. Joseph had the answer for his time, Daniel for his time; we should have answers for our time. God's Word is the answer. As Tim and Bev LaHaye say in their book *The Spirit-Controlled Family*:[15]

> We Christians are not like the secular sophisti-
> cate of our time, who reject all basic guidelines

to life and maintain that each generation must
find for itself the best way to live.

No doubt that is the reason for so much unhappiness in the
average family. Its members are always stumbling around, trying to find the right way to operate. The Spirit-controlled family
is attentive to God's manual on human behavior. The Bible gives
explicit instructions on how the family should function.

There was a time in Israel when everyone did what was right
in his own sight and chaos resulted. Conversely, we have the
word of God, an absolute. First Samuel 15:23 describes their state
by saying, "For rebellion is as the sin of witchcraft, and stubbornness is as iniquity and idolatry."

When King Ahasuerus asked his wife, Queen Vashti to appear
unto him to show her off during a palace celebration, she refused
because she apparently didn't like the party he was having. The
Biblical account can be found in the first chapter of Esther. The
problem begins in verses 10–12.

On the seventh day, when the heart of the king was
merry with wine, he commanded Mehuman, Biztha,
Harbona, Bigtha, and Abagtha, Zethar, and Carcas,
the seven chamberlains that served in the presence
of Ahasuerus the king, to bring Vashti the queen
before the king with the crown royal, to shew the
people and the princes her beauty: for she was fair

to look on. But the queen Vashti refused to come at
the king's commandment by his chamberlains:
therefore was the king very wroth, and his anger
burned in him. (Esther 1:10–12)

In those days, queens and concubines of kings were subject
to the complete will of the monarch as were slaves. For Queen
Vashti to refuse King Ahasuerus before his subjects humiliated
him and because of this, he became very angry. He consulted
with the wise men regarding what should be done to her according to the law.

The wise men concluded that the queen had wronged the
king, the princes, and all the other people in the kingdom. They
believed that when her action became known, other women
would disobey their husbands, and they predicted much con-
tempt and wrath throughout the empire if she went unpunished.
So, to avoid all the confusion and trouble that her rebellion would
create in other women, it was decided that the king should put
her away and choose another queen. This would stop the rebellion that could be the result in the other homes.

The law was made that Vashti should never come before the
king again, and every man should rule his own house. Today, you
don't hear this order taught any more, but it is God's way. There
are many Vashtis in the world and in the Church—women who
refuse to obey their husbands—but they are wrong and are not
pleasing in the sight of God. This woman's actions are an example

of rebellion. It may be politically incorrect, but it is nonetheless the word of God. Look at Romans 13:1–3 for example:

> Let every soul be subject unto the higher powers. For there is no power but of God: the powers that be are ordained of God. Whosoever therefore resisteth the power, resisteth the ordinance of God: and they that resist shall receive to themselves damnation. For rulers are not a terror to good works, but to the evil. Wilt thou then not be afraid of the power? do that which is good, and thou shalt have praise of the same. (Romans 13:1–3)

We have too much disrespect for authority in this world today. Listen to the late-night talk shows. The monologues are rife with jokes about public officials. We have come a long way in the media even in just the past thirty years. According to insider reports, there seems to be not much difference in lifestyles between Kennedy and Clinton. However, no one was writing about or making jokes about President Kennedy's exploits, but President Clinton's scandals are the subject of conversations among elementary school children. It is obvious that respect for high offices has diminished drastically.

Nevertheless, we still must have leaders and they must maintain a level of respect in order to be able to do their jobs effectively. We define the higher powers in the name of government (president, governor, etc.) and church (bishop, pastor, etc.), so we must recognize that the higher power in the home is the husband.

> For the husband is the head of the wife, even as Christ is the head of the church: and he is the savior of the body. Therefore as the church is subject unto Christ, so let the wives be to their own husbands in every thing. (Ephesians 5:23–24)

You just read that the word of God says that the wife should obey her husband in all things. Some women say, "When that man obeys God, then I'll obey him." This is to say if the man is not right with God in her judgment, she will not obey him. Two wrongs don't make a right. Besides, the Bible outlines an eight-point prescription to win a husband to God—and rebellion is not listed as one of the ways.

> Likewise, ye wives, be in subjection to your own husbands; that, if any obey not the word, they also may without the word be won by the conversation of the wives; while they behold your chaste conversation coupled with fear. Whose adorning let it not be that outward adorning of plaiting the hair, and of wearing of gold, or of putting on of apparel; but let it be the hidden man of the heart, in that which is not corruptible, even the ornament of a

meek and quiet spirit, which is in the sight of God of great price. For after this manner in the old time the holy women also, who trusted in God, adorned themselves, being in subjection unto their own husbands: even as Sara obeyed Abraham, calling him lord: whose daughters ye are, as long as ye do well, and are not afraid with any amazement. (1 Pet 3:1–6)

The eight ways to win a husband to God are:

1. Submit,

2. Obey the Word,

3. Have chaste conversation,

4. Let not the outward adorning be the chief aim in life,

5. Let the inner man be adorned more than the outward man,

6. Trust in God (be a holy woman),

7. Do well,

8. Live faithful to your husband, (so there be no fear of being found guilty of infidelity).

If husbands will not hear the preaching of the Gospel, they will hear the preaching of the chaste behavior of their wives. The Greek word for conversation is *anastrophe* which means "conduct or manner of life." If the wife will conduct herself in chastity, in reverence to her husband, and in fear of God, the husband may be won to Christ.

I like the Old Testament example retold in the New Testament about Abraham and Sarah. In 1 Peter 3:6, Sarah is spoken of as being the mother of many daughters who walk in her footsteps. She called Abraham "Lord." Today's Christian women are Sarah's daughters and are instructed to esteem their husbands highly and not to give way to fear. Today's women cannot allow themselves to get tired of doing right by their husbands because they will reap benefits by holding on.

After the rebellion of Vashti and the making of the new law stating that every man should rule his own house, the wrath of the king subsided and he remembered Vashti and the decree against her. The servants of the king laid before him the new plan for finding a queen—the beauty contest. The winner of this contest, the maiden who pleased the king, would become queen instead of Vashti.

The king was pleased with the plan. The most beautiful and talented virgins from all over the kingdom would be brought to him and he would choose a new queen.

> Now in Shushan the palace there was a certain
> Jew, whose name was Mordecai, the son of Jair,
> the son of Shimei, the son of Kish, a Benjamite;
> who had been carried away from Jerusalem with
> the captivity which had been carried away with

Jeconiah king of Judah, whom Nebuchadnezzar the king of Babylon had carried away. And he brought up Hadassah, that is, Esther, his uncle's daughter: for she had neither father nor mother, and the maid was fair and beautiful; whom Mordecai, when her father and mother were dead, took for his own daughter. So it came to pass, when the king's commandment and his decree was heard, and when many maidens were gathered together unto Shushan the palace, to the custody of Hegai, that Esther was brought also unto the king's house, to the custody of Hegai, keeper of the women. (Esther 2:5–8)

Esther was brought to the king's house to enter the contest to determine who was the most talented virgin in all the empire. This was the first and only beauty contest in the Bible.

This story, contrasting Vashti with Esther, should be a warning to all wives who are engaged in rebellion. The first part of 1 Samuel 15:23 says, "For rebellion is as the sin of witchcraft, and stubbornness is as iniquity and idolatry." In context, Samuel was rebuking Saul and said that because Saul had rejected the word of the Lord, God had rejected him from being king. You cannot sin and *not* lose. Adam and Eve lost the Garden of Eden because of sin. The devil lost his position in Heaven because of sin and was kicked out. You cannot sin and keep status. The wages of sin is death. Death will happen to a happy marriage if you allow sin to enter. Vashti lost her kingdom because of stubbornness—maintaining a wrong position and refusing to change her mind in spite of corrective truth. The strict definition of iniquity—self-indulgence—is nothing more than rebellion and rebellion grieves the Holy Spirit. (See Isaiah 63:10.)

I heard a speaker once say, "If the devil is against me, I can pray to God against the devil; but if God is against me, then who can I pray to against God?" You get the point? Thirteen times in the book of Judges, whenever Israel rebelled against God, God raised up other nations to carry them away captive to be punished. So God is not just sitting in heaven, passively looking at your rebellion and not moving toward action. He is slow and merciful only to give *you* a chance to repent. He is a slow-walking God, but when He moves, oh boy! You don't want to fall into the hands of an angry God.

While I am writing this book, I am witnessing a case where this friend of mine is in the middle of a divorce. I talked with him at length and found him to very truthful and sincere. He is about fifty years old and he's tired. I can see it in his eyes. His story is not unique, for there are thousands who are tired of not having a good marriage. For 27 or more years, he has been in an unsuccessful marriage. They stay in the same house and sleep in the same bed, but nothing good is happening. Being a minister of the gospel makes his divorce very hard for some to understand, but ministers are not exempt from this reality of divorce or any other trouble. Job said a man that is born of a woman is but a few days and is full of trouble. That means the minister is included.

My friend's case is like many others. Sometimes you can be with someone and yet be alone. In one place in Scripture, for example, it states that Jesus was alone praying, his disciples with him. Alone and they were "with him." Did you get that? Physically they were together, but actually they were miles apart. There are marriages like this. There are many people who assume that our physical presence in a group means that we are together, but this is not so sometimes.

Let's define "together." It means to be united by agreement into a harmonious working association, based upon a common understanding of the purpose, objectives, aims, and goals of the unified act or program, as well as the duties, functions, obligations, relationships, and responsibilities of each partici- pant who works within, contributes to, and benefits from the total operation.

The question then is: "How can two people not get along if they say that they are Christians, they believe in the same God and Jesus, and claim that the Holy Spirit is dwelling in their lives?" The answer is the same as I stated above—self-indul- gence, which is rebellion. When one or both parties are not con- verted to the idea of practicing the whole truth, the word of God in its entirety, the marriage will fail. Someone is in rebellion.

There has to be a new center between the two and the new center must be Jesus. It's not the husband or wife who is the absolute wisdom of God. It's the Word of God, Jesus the Word made flesh. Amos 3:3 says, "Can two walk together, except they be agreed?" It is important to walk in agreement for the Lord to bless that marriage.

Jesus said, in Matthew 18:19–20, "Again I say unto you, that if two of you shall agree on earth as touching any thing that they shall ask, it shall be done for them of my Father which is in heaven. For where two or three are gathered together in my name, there am I in the midst of them." So if there is no agreement, then there is no answer to prayer and no Jesus present.

So you see, agreement is the remedy for rebellion. How do we then come to this togetherness, this agreement we are talking about in relationships? E. Stanley Jones says there are five stages by which we establish a relationship.[16]

Stage One: *Drawing Near:*

> The indecisive, uncertain stage where we alternately want to, and do not want to, give ourselves to the other person. It is the stage of exploration. I say that is the time of dating. Dating is a prolonged interview, and you can change your mind.

Stage Two: *Decision:*

> The mind ceases to alternate; it is made up.

Stage Three: *Surrender:*

> This is the stage of actual surrender of the self to the other. There is nothing weighted out or measured up, nothing that the eye can see, but inwardly you say, "That person has my heart— he/she has me."

Stage Four: *Taking the Gift:*

> This is the stage when you take the gift of the self of the other. It's the stage of appropriation, of acceptance of the other person as your gift. There is a merging of the selves; inward union takes place.

Stage Five: *Growth:*

> In this stage, there is a blending of will with will, mind with mind, being with being, that will go down through the years.

These are the stages through which we pass in setting up a beautiful human relationship. Some have not gone past the fourth stage—the stage of acceptance. Sometimes we do not know what we are accepting. We need to get to stage five and grow together.

What do we mean when we say "grow?" To grow means to increase in knowledge, quality, stature, beauty, and effectiveness. This produces the characteristics, functions, benefits, and results that have been predestined, planned, designed, or set to be achieved and attained by those who are participants in the progressive process of ever-changing life situations.

It is a problem when both the husband and wife refuse to make a commitment to grow together. Both parties have to make a conscious decision to participate in the growth process. A house that is divided cannot stand. Where there is unity there is strength. I read once that life is what happens after you plan to be successful. Healthy growth will not just happen without help from both parties.

Once I talked more to this friend of mine who is getting divorce, I realized his plight was more complicated than just the fact that he and his wife couldn't get along. He told me that his uncle's influence had a great deal to do with his marrying this young lady. They lived in the same city, went to the same church, and because of expedience, he passively married her instead of marrying the one he really wanted and loved. He had known the woman he married only three months. How can you really know a person in three months well enough to marry him or her? The way things went for them during their marriage, it is obvious that they didn't know each other well enough.

Who knows? Perhaps King Ahasuerus passively married Vashti. Nevertheless, it is true that we sometimes passively end up with Leah instead of Rachel. In Genesis 29, we have the story of Jacob, Leah, Rachel, and Jacob's cunning Uncle Laban. Let's take up the narrative at verse 16:

And Laban had two daughters: the name of the elder was Leah, and the name of the younger was Rachel. Leah was tender eyed; but Rachel was beautiful and well favoured. And Jacob loved Rachel; and said, I will serve thee seven years for Rachel thy younger daughter. And Laban said, It is better that I give her to thee, than that I should give her to another man: abide with me. And Jacob served seven years for Rachel; and they seemed unto him but a few days, for the love he had to her. And Jacob said unto Laban, Give me my wife, for my days are fulfilled, that I may go in unto her. And Laban gathered together all the men of the place, and made a feast. And it came to pass in the evening, that he took Leah his daughter, and brought her to him; and he went in unto her. (Genesis 29:16–23)

Back in those days, the bride was always veiled and the bridechamber dark. With Leah being brought to him in the evening darkness, it is possible that such a deception could have passed the attention of Jacob. Laban shrugged off his little deception simply by explaining that it was customary that the older sister should marry before the younger. The deception meant that Jacob had now passively married Leah, a woman he didn't really love.

I wonder how many men awaken the morning after the wedding to a Leah instead of a Rachel? The veil covered the true identity of Leah. The darkness, in Biblical terminology, means evil and ignorance, so it was evil for Laban to have deceived Jacob no matter what the customs were. Many times, we meet people who seem to be wonderful in the beginning of the relationship, during the trying-to-get-to-know-you period. They put on a front, a mask, a façade—an imposing appearance concealing something inferior. In Leah's case, she was not Jacob's choice, and she also was covering the fact that she had tender eyes or dull eyes, which means she was ugly.

I must say at this point, some people may be pretty on the outside and ugly on the inside. I think the point about Leah was the covering of a perceived weakness. Although she was following the custom and the desire of her father to marry a man who didn't love or prefer her, the deception was still wrong. She suffered rejection. She was not preferred.

My friend told me that the honeymoon night was a disaster. The real person was revealed. In the bed, he started playing with her to get her to relax. He pinched her on the arm and she got angry and hurt from a little pinch. The level of her reaction was totally out of proportion to the pinch. Now this man who I am talking about is a real gentleman and has never hit a woman in his life. After a thorough investigation, he found out that she had been abused by a man in her family—a low-down dog. Her scars for life were hidden until that night of the honeymoon. Now, even after twenty-seven years, she still talks about that little pinch. She never got over her childhood scars that left her wounded for life.

Thus, she became very timid and afraid of men. She was anti-male authority. She became bitter against men and a prime candidate for the Jezebel Spirit, witchcraft, and anti-God order. The Jezebel Spirit comes upon women who have been abused by male authority. I don't know of any abuse worse than sexual abuse. It scars the victim for life. My friend says his wife was abused and refused to let it go or be healed by the word of God or even to seek psychological help.

We all need to be healed of our hurts of the past because as someone has said, "Hurting people hurt other people." I often say, "Don't let your past abort your future." You can't do anything about your past, but you can do something to impregnate your present and give birth to a healthy future. People who have been hurt sometimes inure it—that is, they endure the hurt without expectation of the hurt ever ending. They remain victims. We call that "Victim Consciousness." It's like the commercial that says, "I've fallen and I can't get up."

I hope and pray that this friend and his wife will find healing and closure because it is so sad. The children suffer in cases of divorce. They can become insecure about their own lives and relationships.

What can we do about divorce? Well, first we need to pray earnestly. I am not talking about passive praying either. We need to deal with the Achan that is in our camp. Joshua 7:10–11 tells the story of a man's sin that affected the entire community.

Achan's sin brought a curse on his whole family. The community stoned them to death. In this same way, we must deal with the sin in our camp. I'm not suggesting that we stone anyone who wants to get a divorce. I'm saying that we have to deal with sin that leads to divorce. If we don't deal with it, it will deal with us.

For the wages of sin is death, but the gift of God is eternal life (Romans 3:23). Leave the sins in your life and marriage, move away from those sins. Death does not mean physical only. Death means separation from God and all that is good. The first death is for the spirit to be separated from the body. The second death is to be separated from God eternally, and that is hell.

Some marriages are hellish because there is no God in them. That is the reason we Christians must acknowledge God in all our ways and He shall direct our path. If we apply some of the wisdom from Proverbs to our marriages, it can help us. "The house of the wicked shall be overthrown; but the tabernacles of the upright shall flourish" (Proverbs 14:11). Righteousness exalts a nation but sin is a reproach to any people. Reproach means to be brought down. Exalt means to go up. We need serious healing.

> Good understanding giveth favour: but the way of transgressors is hard. Poverty and shame shall be to him that refuseth instruction: but he that regardeth reproof shall be honoured. The desire accomplished is sweet to the soul: but it is abomination to fools to depart from evil. (Proverbs 13:15, 17, 19)

> Every wise woman buildeth her house: but the fool-
> ish plucketh it down with her hands. (Proverbs 14:1)

The Bible is the book for correction and we need correction in our homes, churches, and the world—period. The spirit
of Elijah is upon me, and when he comes he shall correct all
things. When so many marriages are ending in divorce, we the
church need to address this issue of marriage with some tough
love answers. We don't need euphemistic, slick psychology, but
we need the truth of God's word.

Once in a small Michigan town while conducting a revival
service, a young man gave his heart to Jesus and was saved out
of a life of drugs and alcohol. He joined that particular local
church, and eventually met a young lady and the two were married. Upon my return the following year, the young man introduced me to his new wife and seemed to be happy. But over the
next year or two, he invited me to have dinner at his home. While
sitting at the table, I noticed that his wife looked different—
shorter and with lighter skin coloring. He observed the expression on my face; and it was clear to him that I had remembered
his first wife. We chatted a while longer until I couldn't help but
to ask him about what I was thinking. Now don't get me wrong, I
usually mind my own business, but he and I had developed a
unique "father-in-the-Gospel" type relationship and we had also
become good friends. So I said to him privately, "Your wife looks
different." He chuckled and replied, "She is my new wife." As I
looked at him in shock, my spiritual judgment began to rise. He

said to me, "Let me explain what happened." And he told me the following story:

He and his former wife had one of those typical marriage arguments, if you know what I mean—nothing too serious requiring extreme actions. He explained how he had tried to reconcile with her by apologizing for the misunderstanding, but she refused to forgive and resume their nomal married relationship. She refused him sex, (a form of witchcraft) which went on for weeks and ultimately months with no reconciliation. So he presented his case to the church, and the pastor (being a wise man) instructed the deacon board to go to the home to hear their case. The deacons found nothing about the case that justified her actions and reported their finding to the pastor. The pastor then stated that the two should indeed be reconciled to one another as soon as possible, and gave them a few weeks or months to do so—but to no avail. The pastor went to the home and heard the case, and came to the same conclusion and ordered them to be reconciled, but she continued to refuse. So the pastor presented their case before the church and then released the husband as the scripture states to do in Matthew 18:15–20.

The Contemporary English Bible says in Matthew 18:15–17:

> If one of my followers sins against you, go and point out what was wrong. But do it in private, just between the two of you. If that person listens, you have won back a follower. But if that one refuses to listen, take along one or two others. The Scriptures

teach that every complaint must be proven true by
two or more witnesses. If the follower refuses to listen to them, report the matter to the church. Anyone who refuses to listen to the church must be
treated like an unbeliever or a tax collector.

And the *God's Word to the Nations Bible* puts it this way:

If a believer does something wrong, go, confront
him when the two of you are alone. If he listens to
you, you have won back that believer. But if he does
not listen, take one or two others with you so that
every accusation may be verified by two or three
witnesses. If he ignores these witnesses, tell it to
the community of believers. If he also ignores the
community, deal with him as you would a heathen
or a tax collector. I can guarantee this truth: Whatever you imprison, God will imprison. And whatever you set free, God will set free. I can guarantee again that if two of you agree on anything here
on earth, my Father in heaven will accept it. Where
two or three have come together in my name, I am
there among them (Matthew 18:15–20).

Chapter Five

The Sophisticated Lady: "Mrs. Far Above Rubies"

Who can find a virtuous woman? For her price is far above rubies. I like what Bishop T. D. Jakes says in his book *The Lady, Her Lover, and Her Lord*:[17]

A truly good woman is a wife before she is married. Neither bridal showers nor books can produce in her what has not been inbred. There is within her the unique gift of nurturing that makes her exemplary. She is a carefully calculated mix of strength and vulnerability. Refined and fragile, strong and stable. She is a giving woman, whose life's goal reaches far beyond her own need for fulfillment and anchors in the warm feeling that erupts from touching others.

There is far more required to be a wife than merely being a woman. Every woman is not a wife. Hence, the Scripture declares, 'whoso findeth a wife, findeth a good thing.' That scripture would be ridiculous if the issue were only about finding a woman. No one needs to look far to find a woman. It is the pursuit of a wife that is a challenge, as challenging as digging through a mountain of stones to find a diamond. And like a high-quality gem, those characteristics have to be inherent to a woman. They can't be bought or learned. They can't be forced or formulated. A good wife is a diamond, a treasure that must be mined. Anything else is just a rhinestone. Many foolish men have plunged headlong into the ditch of despair trying to create a jewel from a common rock.

Thank you Bishop Jakes!

Proverbs 19:14 says, "A prudent wife is from the Lord." *Prudent* means "wise, exercising good judgment in practical matters." Foolish and unwise women are not from God. A wife is the anthropomorphism of expedience and romanticism that God wants in a man's life. Anthropomorphism means attributing physical attributes to God, a spirit. God manifested His love through Jesus, and so God uses the woman to manifest that special love—agape mixed with eros. Eros is supported by agape, which is Divine love. Eros means romance. The virtuous woman is a crown to her husband, but she that makes him ashamed is as rottenness in his bones.

I once knew a man who was unwise in choosing a wife. This man was very naive to say the least. The woman he should have married, he didn't, and lives to regret it. The woman he married pursued him, used tricks to get him and even threatened suicide. Already engaged to the virtuous woman, on the day of the wedding, he never showed up. Needless to say, the bride never recovered. This man was in Las Vegas with the other woman and married her instead. It was the mistake of his life. His career suffered severely because of his foolish mistake. Many walked away from him and never forgave him. To make a long story short, what he thought was a blessing turned into a nightmare. She became rebellious, wouldn't feed him or give him due benevolence. She was a stately and attractive woman, but he soon contracted cancer in the bones with great pain and eventually died. A foolish woman will destroy you in the process.

But God gives us only good. "Whoso findeth a wife findeth a good thing and obtaineth favor of the Lord." Note that she's called a good thing. In Luke 11:11–13 Jesus asks, "If a son shall ask bread of any of that is a father, will he give him a stone? Or if he ask a fish, will he for a fish give him a serpent? Or if he shall ask an egg, will he offer him a scorpion? If ye then, being evil, know how to give good gifts unto your children, how much more shall your heavenly Father give the Holy Spirit to them that ask him?"

And look also to James 1:17, "Every good gift and every perfect gift is from above, and cometh from the Father of light, with whom is no variableness, neither shadow of turning. *Variableness* means "tendency to change." Proverbs 10:22 says, "The blessing of the Lord, it maketh rich and he addeth no sorrow with it." Did you get that, "no sorrow with it?" When you get married, life ought to get better. I know the infamous marriage vows say for better or for worse, but the Bible says that working together makes it better.

My wife and I once conducted a marriage seminar in Arizona and we had the men fill out a questionnaire. One of the questions that was asked was, "What bothers you the most?" And of the men, most of them, if not all, answered that their wives didn't know how to talk to them, meaning they did not speak to them with respect. Proverbs 31:26 says, "She openeth her mouth with wisdom, and in her tongue is the law of kindness." She speaks graciously. There's no clamor in her mouth.

I think we all can use better communication skills. Proverbs 15:1–2 says, "A soft answer turneth away wrath, but grievous words stir up anger. The tongue of the wise useth knowledge aright, but the mouth of fools poureth out foolishness." Someone wrote a poem that says, "Sticks and stones may break my bones, but words will never hurt me." That is probably one of the biggest lies ever told. It is said that it takes seven positive words to ease one negative word. Life and death is in the power of the tongue according to Proverbs 18:21. We must guard our tongue, for James 3 says, "And the tongue is a fire, a world of iniquity; so is the tongue among our members that it defileth the whole body, and setteth on fire the course of nature, and it is set on fire of hell."

Proverbs 9:13 declares that, "The foolish woman is clamorous, she is simple and knoweth nothing." She is 1) clamorous: one in continual uproar, noisy, boisterous; 2) simple: silly, easily seduced (2 Timothy 3:6); 3) knoweth nothing: knows no shame, utterly ignorant and depraved. Just recently a friend of mine told me of an incident that occurred on his job. A coworker's wife came on the job with much clamor demanding that the co-worker "come out right now" to see what she wanted. My friend observed that it was so embarrassing to actually see someone's wife acting in such a disgraceful manner.

Solomon said that "it is better to dwell in the corner of the housetop, than with a brawling woman in a wide house" (Proverbs 21:9). He also said, "It is better to dwell in the wilderness, than with a contentious and angry woman." (Proverbs 21:19) The Bible describes the characteristics of a foolish woman in Proverbs 9:13–18 and describes a virtuous woman in Proverbs 12:4: "But she that maketh ashamed is as rottenness in his bones."

What has women meant to men? She is the synonym of all that is holy in a relation—a synonym of all that is encouraging, stimulating, and soothing in life's stress and sorrows.

Woman—God's loveliest gift to man. God pity the man who, in the dark hour of his dissolution, has no woman's hand to wipe away the death damp from his brow, or to smooth his pillow, and no woman's voice to whisper sweet words of cheer and comfort into his fast dulling ear.

Woman—synonym of home and love, of wifehood, or motherhood, of sisterhood, of daughterhood.

Woman—synonym of all gentleness, of charm, of winsomeness, of heart ease, of sacrificial service.

Woman—the uncomplaining bearer of burdens, the partner of pain and pleasure alike, the keeper of the mysteries of life, the fount of joy, the confidant of weakness and sorrow, the sharer of tears and laughter.

Woman—she means to the race all that men's hearts have yearned for, in rest from labor, in refuge from defeat, in comfort from sorrow, in understanding and encouragement, in reproach, in cheer, and in struggle.

That's why this book is so necessary. We have hens crowing and roosters that are no longer in control. We need a healing of correction.

The Who-woman who is ready to be a What-wife is described in the Bible. Proverbs 31:10–31 depicts thirty-one characteristics of a virtuous woman. The Hebrew word for virtuous is *chayil,* which means "strong in all moral and mental qualities" as described in verse 10. These virtuous characteristics are listed below:

1. Morally perfect (verse 10),

2. Invaluable (verse 10),

3. Trustworthy (verse 11),

4. Inherently good and true (verse 12),

5. Ingenious—proficient (verse 13),

6. Thrifty—laborious (verse 14),

7. Dutiful—considerate (verse 15),

8. Versatile—judicious (verse 16),

9. Tireless—healthy (verse 17),

10. Joyful—efficient (verse 18),

11. Watchful—cautious (verse 18),

12. Thrifty—skillful (verse 19),

13. Charitable—benevolent (verse 20),

14. Generous—merciful (verse 20),

15. Fearless—provident (verse 21),

16. Clever at decorating—furnishing (verse 22),

17. Refined in taste (verse 22),

18. Respected—popular (verse 23),

19. Industrious—prosperous (verse 24),

20. Dependable—honest (verse 25),

21. Confident—hopeful (verse 25),

22. Wise—discreet (verse 26),

23. Kind—understanding (verse 26),

24. Prudent—practical (verse 27),

25. Energetic—ever active (verse 27),

26. An ideal wife and mother (verse 28),

27. Honored by her family (verses 27–28),

28. Excels in virtue (verse 28),

29. God-fearing—humble (verse 30),

30. Deserving—successful (verse 31),

31. Honored by the public (verse 31).

Five things said of this woman's husband:

1. He has absolute confidence in her faithfulness (verse 11),

2. He knows she will not be a waster, so he has no need for spoil of his neighbor to supply his house (verse 11),

3. He is blessed by her tireless industry all the days of his life (verse 12),

4. He is exalted as a ruler with the elders at the gate (verse 23),

5. He praises her virtues and blessings to others (verse 28).

A New Testament Picture of Mrs. Far-Above-Rubies

"Mrs. Far-Above-Rubies" lives at Godly house, on the Way of Holiness, in Blessing Town.

The house is built on the Rock of Ages, over which the way of Holiness runs, leading to the Celestial City.

The house overlooks the boundless sea of "the riches of grace" and as it is built foursquare on the rock, the "Sun of Righteousness" is always shining in through one or more of the windows, which are called "praying without ceasing," "rejoice evermore," "in everything give thanks," and "quench not the Spirit."

The house is built with the exceeding great and precious promises of the Scriptures, Jesus Christ Himself being the Chief Cornerstone.

The rooms are lighted with "the light of the knowledge of the glory of God in the face of Jesus Christ."

The house is well furnished with "every good and perfect gift from above." The servants of the house are "Goodness and Mercy" and they are such faithful servants that they follow Mrs. Far-Above-Rubies all the days of her life.

The wholesome diet of the house is the Bread of Life and the water of life, and the milk and honey and corn and wine of Canaan; and truly their mouths are satisfied with good things!

In the garden of the house there grows the fruit of the Spirit —love, joy, peace, long-suffering, gentleness, goodness, faith, meekness, temperance and the fragrant aroma which is exhaled from these fruits and flowers of the garden pervades the whole atmosphere of the place. Yea, this is where Mrs. Far-Above-Rubies lives.

> Her Value – "Her price is far above rubies."
>
> Her Praise – "They arise and call her blessed."
>
> Her Pre-eminence – "But thou excellest them all."
>
> Her Secret – "A woman that feareth the Lord."

The Twentieth-Century Woman of Proverbs

An excellent wife is hard to find. She cannot be bought with expensive jewels or fancy sports cars. Her inner beauty cannot be purchased—it is far greater than money can buy. Her husband trusts her with all of his possessions. He is not concerned that she will drain the checkbook or run up the charge account for her own whims. Rather, she will help to save and economize in order to establish financial security.

> She is a devoted helpmate for his good, a "responder" to his love, one who lives for his fulfillment.

> She decorates the home, keeps the house tidy, and even mops the floor with a song in her heart and praise on her lips.

> She shops wisely at the local supermarket and fresh-vegetable stands for the best buys in food and provides well-balanced nutritious meals that are attractively served.

> She rises early in the morning and serves a good breakfast to her husband and children before driving her children to school and starting her day's schedule.

> She holds home Tupperware parties. From the money she earns, she pays her children's tuition for a Christian education.

She goes to the local health club and exercises her body to keep physically fit and strong.

She senses when her muscles are well toned, because she keeps up with the busy pace of her family well into the evening.

She picks up her needlepoint when she sits down, and keeps her hands busy.

She makes time to assist those who are needy, making soup and casseroles for the sick neighbors and arranging time for volunteer charity work for the poor.

She is a season ahead, planning what warm winter clothes will be needed for the family before the snow begins to fall.

She selects her own wardrobe carefully and is well-groomed in modest apparel. She is not seen outside her home with curlers in her hair, nor does she dress to gain attention.

Her husband is a respected businessman among the leaders of the community.

She operates a ladies boutique from her home (some might term it a "garage sale"), selling some of the lovely articles that she has created.

Charm and self-confidence are her characteristics, and she faces the future with joy and hope.

She speaks with wisdom for studying the Word of God, and her life is an example of kindness to others.

She manages her home with great care and does not sit around idly, watching TV or chatting with her friends on the telephone.

Her children love and respect her, and her husband sings her praises, saying: "You, my darling, are the greatest woman God could have given me."

A charming and beautiful woman can be deceiving, but a woman who reveres the Lord shall be praised.

Her children and her community, who know her well, will see all that she has done and will admire and praise her.

Did you catch the theme, which runs through every activity of the Proverbs woman? Her career is centered in home and family. Everything she does is to better her home and improve the family. She is the "weaver" who intertwines the different threads of the home to produce the beautiful fabric—her family. What a rewarding career—for in the end they rise up and praise her.

Here are some of her characteristics as a home manager: reflector of inner beauty as developed from walking with God, trustworthy partner, careful budgeter rather than a spendthrift, submissive wife, committed helpmate, tender lover, cheerful homemaker, tidy housekeeper, interior decorator, purchasing agent, alert manager of her time, creative cook, chauffeur, businesswoman, wise investor of money, physical-fitness expert, maker of hand-stitchery, volunteer worker, compassionate neighbor, wardrobe planner, clothes designer, wife of a busy husband, creative seamstress, student of the Word, one who daily walks with the Lord an example of a gracious and godly woman.

Her husband has assigned her the management of the home—an area in which to make decisions and sharpen her wits. She certainly need not feel inferior or suppressed. In fact, at times she may feel that is more than she can handle, or she may look upon it as the exciting challenge in life that she was seeking.

The success of the home manager depends upon her attitude of heart toward the job. The real wife works for others willingly and cheerfully from the heart. She imports and exports. If she buys anything, she sells a sufficient amount from her own manufacture to pay for it. She is not afraid to venture into new business to provide for her growing family.

She keeps herself and family in perfect health with proper food and clothing. She has coverings, carpeting and furnishings for her station in life. Her clothing shows marks of refinement and luxury.

Her husband is known and respected in public and has a place of authority among the elders of the land. He is respected not only for his position, but because he is the husband of a woman justly held in universal esteem.

She opens her mouth and speaks wisdom. Kindness is the grace of her lips. She is wise and intelligent and highly cultured in mind and manners. She is graceful and even-tempered in all her ways.

There are few managing women who are not lords over their husbands, tyrants over their servants and haughty toward their neighbors. She is an excellent example of a meek and quiet spirit (1 Peter 3:1–8). She manages her household with economy and discretion. Her children behave well and none keep company with persons of unclean and immoral habits.

She instructs her house in practical religion and industry and sets them an example of godliness, diligence in business and untiring improvement of mind, soul and body. Knowing that idleness leads to vice, she sees that everyone has his own work to perform, and his proper share in food, raiment and other necessities befitting such a household in society. She sees to it that a good education comes next to divine experiences and leads her household to God and His ways. Her children are well-trained and rise up to call her blessed. She excels all other women in wife-hood, motherhood, religion, and industry. Grace of manner is deceitful and beauty of form and features will fade, but the woman who fears the Lord shall be praised. Give such a woman praise and acclaim in the public and render her the fruit of her hands.

Let's end this chapter with a word about the wife as lover. Now, the Bible does not say much to wives about loving their husbands, yet husbands are commanded several times to love their wives. The woman seems to have an emotional nature that makes it easier for her to love. The husband apparently possesses a one-track mind, which can get involved in his business, sports, or other activities, and thus he needs to be reminded to love his wife. She can assist the husband in remembering that he is to love her by being as neat and attractive as possible. Love is not a one-sided affair. It develops out of mutual esteem and admiration for one another.

As that feeling grows, it can be expressed beautifully by the intimacy of the act of marriage. The wife need not be afraid to enjoy this relationship with her husband for it is designed by God. The Creator said that it was not good for Adam to be alone, so He created Eve and said that they were to become one flesh. Normally the woman is a "responder" to her husband's love, but it is in God's order for her to be the initiator from time to time.

According to 1 Corinthians 7:3–4, "Let the husband render unto the wife due benevolence: and likewise also the wife unto the husband. The wife hath not power of her own body, but the husband: and likewise also the husband hath not power of his own body, but the wife." Wives, use this incredible power you have over your husband's body. I guarantee you, he will be well pleased and so will you.

Here are some ways a wife can please her husband:

1. Ask, don't whine, demand, or beg.
2. Compliment him often.
3. Brag about him to your friends.
4. Prepare his favorite dinner and have it ready on time.
5. Draw a scented candlelight bath for him.
6. Buy him gifts for no special reason.
7. Make his surroundings peaceful.
8. Organize his drawers and closet.
9. Keep yourself clean and well-groomed.
10. Surprise him with a manicure and pedicure.
11. Take his mother to lunch or give her a call.
12. Use candlelight for dinner.
13. Laugh with him, never at him.
14. Keep your bedroom experiences exciting.
15. Be considerate of his idiosyncrasies.
16. Don't try to change him.
17. Be confident and self-sufficient.
18. Cheer him on at his sports activities.

19. Tell him a story or read to him aloud.

20. Give him a back, head, or foot massage.

21. Write love notes and hide them in his personal things.

22. Believe the best for him.

23. Use your skills to help him plan his career and make his career moves.

24. Watch TV with him.

25. Don't gossip, nag, or complain.

26. Have his favorite photo blown up and framed.

27. Clean his smudgy glasses with glass cleaner.

28. Notice when his grooming supplies are wornout or used up and replace them.

29. Ask him to teach you something and take a real interest in learning it.

30. Encourage him in all things.

31. Be spontaneous and exciting in everyday life.

32. Notice what's new about him.

33. Learn to be a good cook, keep the kitchen clean and the cupboards full.

34. Wear his favorite perfume.

35. Tell him a story in which he is the hero.

36. Be cheerful when you do not get your own way.

37. Take him on a date.

38. Remind him of his accomplishments.

39. Love him for who he is.

40. Limit your time on the phone.

41. Warm his towel in the dryer while he showers and have it waiting for him when he steps out.

42. Be courteous.

43. When he's speaking, give him your full attention and really listen.

44. Fix his favorite beverage and bring it to him.

45. Cherish your time together.

46. Encourage him to stay within his budget.

47. Cut out articles from the newspaper he'll be interested in.

48. Write him a thank you note.

49. Take him on a picnic.

50. Put the cap on the toothpaste.

51. Respect his privacy.

52. Allow him to have friends.

53. Be faithful always.

54. Respect him in front of your friends.

55. Give him a kiss or a hug for no reason.

56. Treat his associates with respect.

57. Need and heed his advice.

58. Communicate clearly.

59. Don't betray his confidence.

60. Prepare a gourmet lunch for him to take to work.

61. Catalog his CDs or videos.

62. Keep the bathroom clean.

63. Create a dessert and name it after him.

64. Shine his shoes and replace the laces.

65. Keep his clothes cleaned and pressed.

66. Never compare him to anyone.

67. Lip sync his favorite love song—with all the drama you can invent.

68. When you apologize, mean it.

69. Serve him breakfast in bed.

70. Keep a record of his special family commemorations: birthday, graduation, anniversaries and deaths.

71. Keep greeting cards for him to use for his family remembrances.

72. Be his friend.

73. Learn how to tie his tie for him.

74. Even after you've won his heart, flirt with him.

75. Plant a tree in his honor.

76. Praise him to his children.

77. Make him "King for a Day."

78. Be mindful of his moods.

79. Save a few dollars each week for a surprise weekend get-away.

80. Be forgiving and don't hold grudges.

81. Make him a special card.

82. Clean his comb and brush.

83. Pray for him and with him.

PART TWO
THE ROOSTER-
PECKED WIFE

Part Two

The Rooster-Pecked Wife

Proverbs 11:29 says, "He that troubleth his own house shall inherit the wind: and the fool shall be servant to the wise of heart." The man who abuses his wife brings trouble upon his own house and he's considered a fool who needs to be controlled by someone who is wise. That wise controller could be a pastor, counselor, family friend, police officer, or some other government authority. When the rooster (the husband) mistreats the hen (the wife) in any way—physically, mentally, or emotionally— he has participated in spousal abuse. In the animal kingdom, every now and then on the barnyard, a rooster will mistreat a hen. In

these cases, the rooster is destroyed just like when a hen is when she tries to imitate a rooster (see chapter four). A husband's mistreatment of his wife is inexcusable.

Sometimes, Christian women are led to believe that their tolerance for abuse is somehow part of their mandate to be submissive to their husbands. They feel their suffering qualifies as being part of having a meek and quiet spirit. However, this outlook is a perverted understanding of scripture. God never intended for wives to receive abuse from their husbands. On the contrary, husbands are admonished to love their wives as they love their own bodies. A man who loves his wife, loves himself (see Ephesians 5:28). Also, wives are not the only ones who are supposed to be submissive. Ephesians 5, verses 15 and 21 tell us that the husband and wife are admonished to live wisely and be in submission to each other.

Chapter Six

Pecking Too Hard—Domestic Violence/Abuser of Authority

PART TWO: ROOSTER-PECKED WIFE

The article on domestic violence written by Ken Abraham in the May 1998 issue of *New Man* magazine asked the question, "Why would a devoted Christian husband beat his wife? As Paul Luchsinger (the man who is the subject of this article) discovered, the potential for violence exists within every man.

> Happy-go-lucky. Fun-loving. Life of the party. Those
> were just a few of the cheerful words used to

describe Paul Luchsinger. However, few people sus-
pected the hidden, less-friendly reality that hung
over Paul's head like a could of poison gas—"wife
abuse." Paul was a national champion rodeo cow-
boy who made his living "bull-dogging," chasing
down and wrestling steers to the ground. His wife,
Susie, was an award-winning Christian country and
western singer. In public, they stood together on
hundreds of platforms, telling people about the
love of Jesus. But in private, often after a rodeo in
which he had not performed up to his expectation,
and once right before a church service in which
they were to give their testimonies, Paul frequently
vented his anger by shoving and kicking Susie
across the room.

They first met at the 1980 National Final Rodeo in
Oklahoma City where Paul was competing and
Susie's famous sister, country superstar Reba
McEntire, was singing the national anthem. Paul
and Susie fell headlong in love and after a brief
courtship, were married in 1981. By that time, both
Paul and Susie were on the road—Paul traveling
the rodeo circuit and Susie singing back-up with
Reba. The brief amount of time the couple spent
together was usually characterized by newlywed

bliss. By all appearances, they were the perfect couple.

But about six months into their marriage, Paul began to show a different side of his personality. Before long, Paul started showing up backstage at Reba's performances, jealous, angry, and screaming at Susie. Paul's expressions of anger quickly intensified from loud verbal abuse of Susie to knocking doors off hinges, breaking up furniture, and finally, physically abusing his wife. Says Susie, "Before long, he moved to grabbing me and shoving me to the floor, kicking me in the rear and utterly humiliating me by his demeaning words and actions."

"I knew I was wrong," says Paul. "As a man—especially as a Christian man—I knew I was expressing my anger in an inappropriate, sinful way. But while I was doing it, I didn't care. The truth is, it felt good to vent my anger. I loved Susie yet I was oblivious to the pain I was inflicting on her."

Following Paul's angry outbreaks, he cried, apologized, and promised Susie he would change. But after a while, the ugly cycle would repeat itself.

Susie, ashamed and afraid, told no one about what was happening in her household. In late 1986, the occurrences of violence began to spill outside the walls of their home. For the first time, Paul's beatings caused visible marks on Susie's body. Eventually two other people witnessed Paul's violent behavior and confronted him on it. Jim Bode Scott, the man who had led Paul to the Lord, and his wife, Marcie became aware of the domestic violence when Paul threatened Susie at the Scott's home. A former steer wrestler himself, Jim stuck his index finger in Paul's chest and said, "That's not the way to treat a woman, and it's sure not the way God intended marriage to be." Jim embraced Paul in his big arms and said, "Brother, we are going to walk through this together." It was a turning point in Paul's life and in the Luchsinger's marriage.

How can a man in Christ like Paul Luchsinger do such a thing as beat his wife? The answer is, "Iniquity," the hidden sin. The Hebrew word for iniquity is a verb, the part of speech that indicates existence or action. In Arabic, this verb appears with the meaning 'to bend or to deviate from the way.' *Awah* is often used as a synonym of *hata* and both mean 'to sin' as in Psalms 106:6: "We have sinned with our fathers, we have committed iniquity (awah), we have done wickedly."

Paul spoke of the iniquity that he found within his own personality.

> For we know that the law is spiritual: but I am carnal, sold under sin. For that which I do I allow not: for what I would, that do I not; but what I hate, that do I. If then I do that which I would not, I consent unto the law that it is good. Now then it is no more I that do it, but sin that dwelleth in me. For I know that in me (that is, in my flesh,) dwelleth no good thing: for to will is present with me; but how to perform that which is good I find not. For the good that I would I do not: but the evil which I would not, that I do. Now if I do that I would not, it is no more I that do it, but sin that dwelleth in me. I find then a law, that, when I would do good, evil is present with me. For I delight in the law of God after the inward man: But I see another law in my members, warring against the law of my mind, and bringing me into captivity to the law of sin which is in my members. O wretched man that I am! Who shall deliver me from the body of this death? I thank God through Jesus Christ our Lord. So then with the mind I myself serve the law of God; but with the flesh the law of sin. (Romans 7:14–25)

Plato wrote about the tripartite of human nature using the image of the charioteer being pulled apart by his god and bad horses. He thus painted a vivid picture of the internal conflicts often faced by human beings. I see iniquity like a bad dog in a yard with a fence that has a gate. The gate must remain closed or the bad dog will escape and do harm. Your "dog" may be a bad temper, sex, whatever. Men need to control their "dogs." If the "dog" is anger, it very well could break through that gate and attack your wife.

While women use manipulation, men use domination or intimidation. But men, beware of the judgment of God in this matter. Remember, men are supposed to love their wives as Christ loved the Church and as they love themselves. Peter also addressed this matter in 1 Peter 3:7: "Likewise, ye husbands, dwell with them according to knowledge, giving honour unto the wife, as unto the weaker vessel, and as being heirs together of the grace of life; that your prayers be not hindered."

Knowing that the wife is the weaker vessel should give men a clue. Their strength can be used wrongly and if it is, that is not honoring to the wife. The word says that the prayers of the man who does not honor his wife will be hindered. Now who wants to have his prayers hindered? Do you really want to block your communication with God? I don't think so.

Men must also learn how to pray from the model prayer that our Lord taught his disciples. The first part of the prayer is, as E. Stanley Jones suggests, your protocol and realignment. We say,

"Thy will be done on earth as it is in heaven." This is the crux of the prayer. If a man sincerely prays for God's will to be done, he will never mistreat his wife because that is never God's will.

Then we add, "Give us this day our daily bread," and then, "lead us not into temptation, but deliver us from evil." That is the victory part. We need bread, but we also need victory. Victory means progress unhindered reaching your goals. A man can receive victory once and keep from mistreating his wife, but that doesn't mean he won't be tempted to abuse her at another time. I want to wipe away all excuses for our recidivism (repeating the crime). It is necessary to pray for repeated victory over the temptation. Each time the temptation comes, cast it down. In the seventh chapter of Romans, Paul deals with the reality of vacillation, the war inside of us all, but he didn't stop there. He went on to say in the eighth chapter, that there is therefore now no condemnation for those who are in Christ Jesus, who walk not after the flesh, but after the Spirit.

> There is therefore now no condemnation to them which are in Christ Jesus, who walk not after the flesh, but after the Spirit. For the law of the Spirit of life in Christ Jesus hath made me free from the law of sin and death. For what the law could not do, in that it was weak through the flesh, God sending his own Son in the likeness of sinful flesh, and for sin, condemned sin in the flesh: That the

righteousness of the law might be fulfilled in us,
who walk not after the flesh, but after the Spirit.
(Romans 8:1–4)

Paul thanks God Who has given us the victory through our Lord Jesus Christ. So as you can see, men can overcome their propensity to mistreat and intimidate their wives and love them through the power of God. The man who insists on being dominating and rude is the fool of Proverbs 11:29 and is troubling his house.

I have a message I preach entitled "Gone with the Wind." I know that's a famous movie, but I'm speaking of men who trouble their own houses. These men will end up in some restaurant like Denny's, eating with another lonely brother or friend. Just like Adam lost his home in the Garden of Eden because of sin, an abusive man can lose his home.

Let's look at some red flags that could point to abusive tendencies in your dating or marriage relationship. A man should ask himself these questions and if he answers "yes" to any, he has abusive tendencies—that "dog" that needs to be carefully locked behind the gate.

1. Do you try to isolate your mate, making it difficult for her to see family or friends?

2. Do you use intimidation tactics such as standing over her or preventing her from leaving the room?

3. Do you engage in uninvited touching or use coercion to obtain sex?

4. Do you give harsh personal criticisms of your mate, including name-calling and put-downs?

5. Do you attempt to publicly embarrass her?

6. Do you use pressure tactics to control her, including threats to withhold financial support?

7. Do you sabotage your wife's attempts to work outside the home or to be a stay-at-home mom?

8. Do you twist your wife's words to mean something she may not have intended?

9. Do you try to manipulate your children to get them to see things your way?

10. Do you claim to be the absolute authority in the home, refusing to give your wife any say?[18]

What are the responsibilities of the husband? According to Ephesians 5:23–27, he is seen as family leader, ideal lover, father-teacher, provider, family priest, and protector. God's first assignment for the husband is to be the head of the family. As leader, he must be able to give direction for the well being of the family. For that he needs divine wisdom. I love the scripture that says, "O LORD, I know that the way of man is not in himself: it is not in man that walketh to direct his steps. O LORD, correct me, but

with judgment; not in thine anger, lest thou bring me to nothing." (Jeremiah 10:23–24) Acknowledge God in all your ways and
he shall direct your path. (Proverbs 3:6) Men, we need God leading us as we lead our families.

When a man takes a wife, he had better be ready for an awe-
some responsibility. Being a husband myself, I understand that.
Husbands must provide a security clause. He may feel inadequate
or unstable himself. God's personality is described as being that
of a rock. Husbands should express that rock-like personality of
dependability to his wife and children. God's personality is also
described as a tower of refuge. A man should be like a fortress of
protection for his family. They should see him as a sturdy wall
that keeps away all harmful enemies. According to Keith Intrater,
in his book *Covenant Relationships*:[19]

> A man primarily ministers to his wife and chil-
> dren in the area of stability, security, protection,
> and provision. It takes faith for a man to stand in
> his position as the source of security for his fam-
> ily. If a woman acts pushy and manipulative, she
> is often struggling with fear and insecurity. If the
> husband reacts defensively, he will only cause her
> to be more insecure, which will create even more
> pushiness. If the husband remembers to minis-
> ter to his wife's sense of security, she will be able
> to relax. She can then return to him the blessing
> of being a submissive and supportive wife.

Where are the godly men? Psalm 12:1 says, "Help, LORD; for the godly man ceaseth; for the faithful fail from among the children of men." We hope the godly men are in the church. I said once, in a message about men to the women in the congregation, that God even had a hard time himself trying to find a man. He searched the heaven and the earth and then looked under the earth and still couldn't find a man qualified.

In order to be men God can use, men must take on a godly character. They must depend upon God who is able to work in them the will to do and be what they ought to be. I like what Tim and Bev LaHaye say in their book *Spirit-Controlled Family*: "It matters not that she is quick acting and he is passive. She needs a leader."

Genesis 3:16 says a woman's desire shall be to her husband. If he shirks the role of leadership out of neglect or ignorance because he didn't see it in his father or doesn't know the Bible, or has his own personal weakness, he is damning his wife to a lifetime of psychic frustration. Some women gradually become carnal, dominating, neurotic, and obnoxious as the years roll by. It's very difficult for a woman to submit to a man who refuses to lead.

I hear of men who understand baseball, football, basketball, and cars, but they don't understand a thing about their wives. Men can listen to the car and know when the engine is not running right, but they cannot hear what is happening in the hearts and minds of their wives. The introduction to the book *Caring Enough to Hear and Be Heard*[20] speaks to this issue.

My side of the argument is clear. Your side is occasionally confused. My side of the issue is logical. Your side is sometimes irrational. My side of the hassle is justified. Your side is frequently unwarranted. My side of the conflict is crucial. Your side is often unnecessary. My side of the conversation makes sense to me; it is my experience of a vivid slice of human existence. But your side is "the other side." I have not experienced it; I do not understand it.

The art of dialogue is openness to the other side, willingness to enter the other's turf and explore it until it is familiar territory. The heart of dialogue is coming to value a place near the center, on the boundary where the other person's perspective is valued alongside my own. At this point of meeting, I become as concerned for the clarity of the other's stance as for my own; as willing to contribute an argumentative point to the other side as to assert one of my own; as committed to supporting the others' right to be at his or her position as I am to claim my own. Both sides are a gift, a gift to each other in our building responsive communication—a gift of God who calls us to create a community of grace. We as human beings are selfish when it comes to hearing the other person. We hear what we want to hear. Abuse never fosters open and clear communication.

We have discussed physical abuse, but we need to also understand that there is such a thing called mental abuse. To reject the thoughts of another, especially one's wife, is a form of abuse. To not listen when she is trying to express herself, causing her to feel her thoughts are not important, is cruel and abusive. Men sometimes talk to their wives demeaningly and only about stressful matters like bills and problems with the children. Women need their husbands to talk to them about their person.

Wake up, husbands! It's said that relationship is the meaning to life. I will never forget a segment I saw on the Oprah Winfrey Show. A socialite woman had left her rich husband for the garbage man. The rich man had given her everything she needed materially, but he did not give her himself. The garbage man didn't have anything to give her but himself. She left the palace that was a prison for her, for the garbage man.

Who can forget Princess Diana of Wales. Hers was such a sad story. She had everything except real love. That is a classic example of mental abuse. She was never good enough for Prince Charles, no matter how pretty she was, she was not pretty enough. She suffered from low self-esteem. Can you imagine such a woman suffering from low self-esteem? The palace was truly a prison.

I still remember my mother's face. She was abused not only physically but mentally as well. After having five boys and one sweet little girl, she was rejected and put away. My parents were separated most of my life. She died loving a man who didn't love her. She died and never lived.

There are some things that are destroying the potentiality of men who are striving to be good husbands. There are men who are rough and have no tenderness, rude without any politeness. Rudeness is simply an imitation of strength for a weak man. Men must live up to what God expects from husbands.

We know by now the husband is the leader of the family, but he is not a dictator. He's an ideal lover. Husbands, love your wives as Christ loved the Church. Love is not just a feeling. It is a commitment that brings about good feeling. Serve as leader of your wife as Christ is the head of the Church. That means you will have a leadership of love. Our Lord directs us, leads us, makes decisions for us, and takes responsibility for us in a spirit of love and consideration, thinking of good. Husbands, you must love and honor your wives in the same way.

Chapter Seven

The Who Without the What

Now there is at Jerusalem by the sheep market, a pool which is called in the Hebrew tongue Bethesda, having five porches. In these lay a great multitude of impotent folk, of blind, halt, withered, waiting for the moving of the water. For an angel went down at a certain season into the pool, and troubled the water: whosoever then first after the troubling of the water stepped in was made whole of whatsoever disease he had. And a certain man was there, which had an infirmity thirty and eight years. When Jesus saw him lie, and knew that he had been now a long time in that case, he saith unto him, Wilt thou be made whole? The impotent man answered him,

Sir, I have no man, when the water is troubled, to put me into the pool: but while I am coming, another steppeth down before me. (John 5:3-7)

This man paralyzed for 38 years represents the Who without the What. When we say the Who, we are really saying he is without definition. So we are looking for the What, the quiddity, that which makes a thing what it is. The man who was laying by the pool is a Who, not a What.

Notice this man did not have a family and he was not qualified to have a family because he was invalid. We must define ourselves as the What before we can assume the responsibility of husband or wife. Every person is a Who and has value as such, but every person is not the same What. For the purposes of our discussion, every Who-man is not a What-husband, and every Who-woman is not a What-wife.

PART ONE: THE WHO AS HUSBAND

Once a man defines himself as a husband, he is confined to a limited role and must have the potential to bring four things to the relationship: stability, security, protection, and provision. The husband must minister to his wife and children in these areas. If he is not able to do that, then he is just a Who (a man) and not a What (a husband). God deals with the What, the husband role, in marriage.

God wants to join faithful men to virtuous women.

Proverbs 20:6: Most men will proclaim every one
his own goodness: but a faithful man who can find?

Proverbs 25:19: Confidence in an unfaithful man
in time of trouble is like a broken tooth, and a foot
out of joint.

God, who is all knowing, will not give you bad gifts. All good
and perfect gifts come from the Lord. The husband represents
God on earth and God is faithful. God is like a rock in a weary
land, so must the husband be to his wife and family. The man
like God must be a tower of refuge, a fortress or protection for
his family. The Who alone cannot provide this but the What can.

The man at the pool had some sort of paralysis. Isn't it amaz-
ing how the miracles of Christ possess as much illustrative value
as they do evidential significance? We moderns know something
about paralysis. Paralysis is a helplessness. John could scarcely
have illustrated the root causes of spiritual paralysis more clearly
than the way in which he tells the story of this man by the pool
of Bethesda. Looking closely into this story could give us some
insight into men who are 'Whos' but not 'Whats' (husbands).

The man by the pool had lain for thirty-eight years. This suggests the hardening of habit. The man was simply stuck with his
condition—inured to it.

Bill was like the man by the pool. He had been used to
living one way and his marriage demanded that he live another

way. Bill had been brought up by loving parents who catered to his wishes. They did discipline him, but by and large, he got everything he really wanted throughout his childhood, high school, and college years without much effort. In college, he would drop classes he didn't like or ones in which he wasn't doing well. He would rather play in his band than buckle down to course work. Although he had a part-time job that would become full time in his line of work when he graduated from college, he was still taking his time about completing all the necessary course work for graduation. He had not spent his own money to buy his car; his father had bought it for him. He was twenty-five years old and still living at home when he met his fiance.

Bill entered marriage with great intentions, but because he had never been challenged to be his own man, when the time came to shoulder the responsibilities of a wife, children, house, and the normal stresses of life including unexpected twists and turns, he found himself unprepared. He began to do very destructive things including leaving his career, overspending, being emotionally abusive to the children, and physically abusing of his wife. Although prompted by his wife for them to get counseling, neither professional nor spiritual counseling helped. The marriage ended in divorce after 13 years.

Bill was stuck in a condition he couldn't overcome. He simply could not handle what most would consider normal adult responsibilities, mainly because he had not had practice being responsible as a teenager and young adult. He was never forced to face the consequences of his actions and was always bailed out by his parents. He was paralyzed.

Some folks are made to be prodded, pushed, carried, helped, led. Some folks are made to be leaned on, others are perpetual leaners. Sometimes the leaners resent being prodded even though they complain if they are left to themselves. But, in other cases, the sense of personal inadequacy is deep and very painful. They are convinced that no blessing, success, opportunity, or real contribution to the world could ever be within their reach. No initiative any longer stirs. Custom has made them impervious to persuasion, armored against new ideas, fortified against change, and full of reasons for not trying anything new.

There is still hope for Bill though, because there was hope for the man by the pool of Bethesda. When Jesus came along, the man was roused at once. Suddenly, he was no longer inured and complaining. He became aggressively determined to show the Prophet he was no malingerer. He protested his eagerness, if only anyone would help him.

Like other Who's, the man at the pool had to be moved by Jesus Christ before he could dream of becoming a What. It's the command and touch of the Master that makes the difference.

Jesus told the man at the pool to rise up, take up his bed, and walk. Never mind how often he had tried and failed before. It didn't matter that little hope had survived the long frustration. When the Lord commanded the man, he had to take action.

Today, the Lord can speak through sermons, friends, and counselors. Men who want to become What-husbands must put right whatever went wrong, no matter how long ago it happened. Break the fetters of Habit. Bestir the idleness of mind. Have done with the long dependence upon others. The authority you confront in Christ demands implicit obedience. Do not pretend you cannot obey. Your own heart will tell what needs doing. Do it because He tells you to.

Finally, Jesus told the man at the pool to sin no more or a worse thing would come upon him. This suggests some deeper cause of trouble, something in that borderline between mind and soul where either affects the other. Physical symptoms may have a mental cause and mental trouble a physical basis. As in helplessness, Jesus speaks of sin that saps life of energy, usefulness, and hope. A half-forgotten wrong buried deep in the subconscious mind, may turn septic, draining the soul of all health and vigor.

Christians soon discover the virulence of sins unconfessed, of quarrels unreconciled for years, or of failures in duty of love never acknowledged or for which there has been no atonement. Prayer becomes spiritless, worship dull, Christian work mere duty, and religious living an unrewarding ritual, grimly sustained to hide inward disappointment. This too is paralysis; grace no longer enjoyed.

Who-men who want to become What-husbands face a paralysis of the mind, the conscience, and the will. What-husbands yield to the pulse of inflowing divine life that is in contact with the living Christ. It is up to the man if he will be made whole.

We have a new word for a paralysis that is not brought on by a physical illness. We call it being a victim.

In her book entitled *Are You The One For Me?,*[21] Barbara De Angelis, Ph.D. talks about victims consciousness and she asked women in her audience this question, "Are you in love with a victim?" A husband may not be able to be the What his wife wants him to be because he is another kind of What, a What-victim. Here are some common traits of victim consciousness that De Angelis points out:

- Has a hard time receiving love and support,

- Enjoys suffering,

- Holds on to pain, giving the illusion of having power over those who have inflicted hurt,

- Is never satisfied, no matter how much you give,

- Refuses to be cheered up,

- Rarely gets directly angry with you or others; instead, complains or pouts about the situation,

- Won't come right out and tell you what's bothering him, but walks around looking miserable and makes you pull the information out,

- Your love and comfort, no matter how hard you try, doesn't help,

- Always finds something to be upset about. (Rarely have days and weeks gone by without some event that puts him in a bad mood.),

- Has a difficult time making decisions and often spends more time complaining about what might happen than taking action,

- Blames people in the past (parents, ex-mates, friends) for his misfortunes and the way his life has turned out,

- Often feels trapped in circumstances that he feels are the causes of his unhappiness and can see no way out.

Dr. DeAngelis also states that there are many fatal flaws:

1. Addictions,

2. Anger,

3. Victim Consciousness,

4. Control Freak,

5. Sexual Dysfunction,

6. Hasn't grown up,

7. Emotionally unavailable,

8. Hasn't recovered from past relationship,

9. Emotional damage from childhood.

If our boys will ever become men, they must be taught by example to assume the manly responsibility of throwing away those things that are doing none of us any earthly good. We have probably all seen the license plate frame that reads, "The difference between the men and the boys is the size, the look, and the price of their toys." That is a vicious, venomous lie peddled from the pit of perdition. It's cute, but not correct. The list of what real men do is not so easily put into a pop slogan. It is too precious, too valuable, almost sacred. Here are just a few of the hundreds of things real men do. I encourage you to take a pen and paper and expand the list because it is not meant to be exhaustive, but encouraging and enlightening.

24 Things Real Men Do

1. Real men put away toys and pick up tools.

2. Real men do not just play—they pray.

3. Real men do not party—they participate.

4. Real men do not just work out—they work!

5. Real men do not just date—they develop.

6. Real men do not just father a baby—they become a father to the baby.

7. Real men do not just love them and leave them—but they love them and help them . . . bless them and hold them, support them and take care of them.

8. Real men take care of their babies . . . pay their support, and pay it on time, in the right amount, and with some extra thrown in.

9. Real men stand on the Promise instead of the promiscuous.

10. Real men call home and tell their wives if they cannot make it home. They also tell them why.

11. Real men who are married come home at a decent hour because they respect their wives and children.

12. Real men who are single and saved know there is no such thing as safe sex—only saved sex. Any sex without the benefit and blessing of marriage is headed for physical and spiritual disaster.

13. Real men open doors, stand up when a woman enters the room or arrives at the table. This real man always offers the woman his seat.

14. Real men work for their money; boys expect something for nothing.

15. Real men get a job and keep a job; they are providers, protectors and priests.

16. Real men are family men.

17. Real men are faithful to their wives. They realize if they spent as much time on their wives as they do on their

girlfriends, they would have the wives they were making the girlfriends to be.

18. Real men do not do cigarettes, alcohol, or any other drug. They know their bodies are a sacred gift, a temple of the Holy Spirit, and not a place for sin.

19. Real men know that sex is who you are and love is what you do.

20. Real men never lift a hand to women unless they are reaching to Heaven to bless her.

21. Boys talk back to their parents; men take care of their parents.

22. Boys chase girls; men respect sisters.

23. Boys wear hats inside a building; men remove them out of respect for themselves and others.

24. Boys cuss a mile a minute; men guard their tongues.[22]

Part Two: The Who as Wife

There are certain women who can never become good wives. They will never be able to answer, never be able to agree to any man.

Number one is the dominant female. Let's call her Dominant Delilah. That's the woman who runs every aspect of her home *and* her husband. When she does, she's entirely out of character. I do not believe most women want to take the lead, so what is it that causes this domination? Well, she may have a higher IQ than her husband, or she may have a stronger personality. As a result, he may become a little Mr. Milquetoast. I feel sorry when such a marriage takes place today. She becomes frustrated and begins to nag and criticize her husband and find fault with him.

Two girls who had been together in college met years later on the street. One said to the other, "Are you married?"

"Yes."

"Forgive me for laughing, but I remember that when we were in college you used to say you wouldn't marry the most perfect man on earth."

Her curt reply was, "I didn't!"

Some men marry women who are headstrong and competitors with their men. When a woman does this, she loses her femininity. Sometimes after she rules the roost at home, she looks for other worlds to conquer. She becomes involved in clubs—these are the club women we see today. Some even get involved in politics. Others became unusually good businesswomen and launch a career of their own. This is not meant to imply all career women are Dominant Delilahs. Sometimes they come over to the church and try to run the preacher. That's when we preachers have fun.

I remember it was said of Dr. Jim McGinley that when one of these Dominant Delilahs said to him in disgust, "If you were my husband, I'd poison your coffee," his instant reply was, "If you were my wife, I'd drink it!" The dominant female is never prepared to be a real wife.

The second woman is one who is ruled by envy and jealousy. You'll always find that these women are the gossips. So let's call her Gossipy Gussie. I have never yet seen a gossip who had a happy home. These are the frigid women of today. The husband and the children are miserable, and she is incapable of answering or agreeing as a wife. Every church has a few of these. They wreck their own homes, and they attempt to wreck their churches.

The third one is the neurotic woman. Let's call her Hysterical Hortense, or if she's not too extreme, we could call her Nervous Nellie. When she doesn't get her way, she's the one who acts up. Her husband always walks on eggshells. He wasn't quite what she thought he was, and she begins to make him over. I heard of a husband who asked his wife one day, "Why in the world did you ever marry me when you found out there were so many things wrong with me?" She wanted to make him over altogether. What if he doesn't fall into her pattern? She'll give him the silent treatment and pout for days. There will be a tense atmosphere in the home. This woman, of course, is never prepared for marriage at all.

Then there is the woman who marries so that she might have financial security.

We'll call her Gold-Digger Gertie, and unfortunately, there are Christians today who are like that.
May I say this to you, dear ladies, if you are looking for the type of man who can take care of you
financially, you may have peace and security regarding the finances, but you will never know what
real love is, nor the peace and joy of being able to
agree with a husband who really loves you. [23]

So you can marry a who without the what. It is what God
hath joined together. Let no man put asunder.

PART THREE

WHAT GOD HATH

JOINED TOGETHER

Chapter Eight

What Is A Marriage?
Matthew 19:4—6

PART THREE: WHAT GOD HATH JOINED TOGETHER

A marriage is an intimate personal union to which a man and woman consent. It is consummated and continuously nourished by sexual intercourse, and perfected in a life-long partnership of mutual love and commitment.

It is also a social institution regulated by the Word of God and by the laws and customs which a society develops to safeguard its own continuity and welfare.

Nature and Purpose

Marriage is an order of Creation. The Creator made man and woman, displaying His full image only as both man and woman.

Each is made for the other; as both their natures are complementary, and are brought into oneness in marriage, (Genesis 12:26 and Matthew 19:4-6).

Marriage is the sacrament of human society. Husband and wife both share and perpetuate their happiness in having and rearing a family within the sphere of their own love.

The unity of husband and wife is of God's creative will. From Him comes the love and grace which enable them to grow together in life comradeship.

Distinctly, Christian marriage is one in which the husband and the wife covenant together with God and publicly witness their commitment not only to each other but to Him, to the end of that they shall in unity fulfill His purposes throughout life. (I Corinthians 7:39 and II Corinthians 6:14)

Marriage is contracted "in the Lord, " received as divine vocation, acknowledge with humility and thanksgiving, and sanctified by the Word of God and prayer, (1 Timothy 4:4-5).

Marriage is the highest fulfillment of human friendship, and fills the very ideal of human intimacy and mutuality and loyalty.

Man

Man is the only creature who can have marriage instead of mating, for marriage involves commitment for the future and the confidence of permanence. Man also discerns his own loneliness and incompleteness (Genesis 2:18) and the possibility of the complementary nature of marriage—husband and wife both fulfilling that which is lacking in the other.

Sexual Fulfillment

Sex is holy, being the creation and gift of God. It is fulfilled only as regulated by the law of God in marriage. Man and woman were created to complement each other in God's creative process. Man alone can make sex moral, giving it a non-biological meaning, and making it create personal and spiritual values. Love, fidelity and human sexuality, has a dual purpose of communion and reproduction.

Chapter Nine

Unresolved Issues

*. . . and every city or house divided against itself
shall not stand.* (Matthew 12:25b)

Can two walk together except they be agreed?
(Amos 3:3)

Most people's bodies are well able to fend off the common cold. Healthy bodies are equipped with immune systems that immediately begin to fight off any foreign germ or virus that enters. In the case of the common cold, it may take seven to ten days to totally shake the symptoms, but the body handles the problem. However, if the body's immune system has been compromised somehow, for example by the AIDS virus, when confronted with a common cold virus the system would not be able to do its job as well, if at all.

In the same way, the African-American couple enters marriage already at a disadvantage. We have come to understand the deception that was foisted upon the Black family to destroy it and keep the imbalance self-perpetuating. The Lynch system compromised the strong foundation of the African-American family.

Overlaid on top of the forced reversed roles and subsequent rebellious Vashti and anti-male Jezebel spirits are the normal challenges all marriages face. With the handicaps begun by Lynch in mind, let's discuss how the five forces that can lead to isolation even in healthy marriage effect the African-American family.

PART ONE:
FIVE FATAL FORCES DESTROYING ONENESS

Maintaining oneness is a critical issue in marriage. How does an enthusiastic, optimistic, and hopeful marriage turn into a disaster? Couples today are being deceived by five forces that are destroying oneness and leading to isolation in marriage. The five forces are:

1. Difficult adjustments,

2. Acceptance based upon performance,

3. Failure to anticipate selfishness,

4. Failure to work through inevitable difficulties and trials,

5. An extramarital affair for fulfillment outside of marriage.

Force #1: Difficult Adjustments

Difficult adjustments threaten oneness in marriage. The home is at the apex of sociological change and there is little in our culture or world today that encourages marital oneness. Consider the difference almost 200 years has made in the way we view home.

In the 1800s, life in the home was simple—much like *Little House on the Prairie.* The economy, jobs, and roles changed very little. Men worked an 80-hour work week and families were closely knit. The responsibilities were clear and home was the major influence in children's lives. The children were an economic asset—they were producers working on the family farm. Recreation was around the home and everyone participated in creative fun. Community involvement was minimal. The religious life was the main influence to develop the home and church on Sundays was mandatory for almost everyone.

The pattern of authority was patriarchal. The father worked outside the home and the mother kept the home fires burning. Women worked on the farm and in the home in order to survive. Marriage was for security and partners were chosen from among acquaintances. Divorces were frowned upon and roles were clear.

Probably one of the most difficult adjustments back then was realizing that, once you were married, you were the adult who would now have to take on the roles you saw your parents have. Yet, unlike today, this realization seemed to have been much more readily accepted. Even nature, as we have seen, provided the same kind of example; the rooster did the crowing and the hen laid the eggs.

In contrast, we find ourselves at the end of the 1900s, looking at a home that is drastically different from that of the 1800s. In the industrial economy of the '80s and '90s, jobs and roles have changed. Parents often work a 40-hour work week rather than an 80-hour work week, yet seem to have even less time for their children. This has led to a population of irresponsible adults and children. The children are an economic liability instead of an asset, and they make no contribution to the home. Many times, these children will not even wash the dishes or put out the trash. All they do is eat.

Outside interference creeps in, the biggest of which is television. Television is the thief of family time, stealing even the times we eat together. Talking with each other in the home is a thing of the past. A high school teacher interviewed her five English classes only to be shocked to find that less than 5% of each class said they actually ate dinner together as a family.

You may be shocked to know that another outside interference is the church. Yes, the church is responsible for stealing family times together with too many meetings a week. Wow, too much church? "Let your moderation be known."

Couples also marry nowadays for social purposes. They choose partners from any source and the contrasting backgrounds bring about sometimes painful adjustments for a couple in the following areas:

What are our values?

Which religion will we follow?

How will we handle our finances?

What will be our vocations?

How will we raise our children?

How will we handle our aging parents?

How much influence will our extended families
have on our lives?

It surprises many people to learn that different cultures view these issues in sometimes drastically different ways. Couples who come from different cultural backgrounds may face major adjustments when they deal with these issues and these adjustments may not be that easy to make.

Couples now see marriage as temporary from the start. Divorce is an acceptable solution instead of conversion, and divorce can happen when one or both parties refuse to make difficult yet necessary adjustments. Couples don't anticipate having to make changes in their ideas about things such as the roles both should play, the expression of love, and sexual performance. Without making these necessary adjustments toward oneness, isolation is inevitable, separation will follow, and finally there could be divorce.

Force #2: Acceptance Based Upon Performance

The world's plan will undermine the oneness you desire. The world's plan is a 50-50 performance relationship and acceptance is based upon performance—you do your part and I'll do mine. Giving is based upon merit, and acceptance is given when one feels it has been deserved. Motivation for action is based upon how one feels at the time. The world's 50-50 performance relationship is destined to fail because of our inability to meet unreal expectations. It is impossible to know if our mate has met us halfway. There is a tendency to be disappointed in our mates which paralyzes our performance.

The husband expects the wife to act a certain way. When she does, he accepts her. Conversely, the wife expects the husband to act a certain way, and when he does, she accepts him. The problem is, each one's expectations are different and are based on a totally different scale. Therefore, no matter what she does, it's not what the husband expected her to do, so he doesn't give acceptance, and she feels isolated. No matter what he does, it isn't what the wife expected him to do; so she doesn't show him acceptance, and he feels isolated. This isolation can force them apart. What has to happen is for the husband and wife to come together to understand where the other is coming from.

No matter what the proponents of the Women's Liberation Movement have tried to sell you, men and women are *not* the same. They are not equal. They are like interlocking puzzle pieces—although they are shaped differently and have differing patterns, they fit together perfectly. They complement each other.

I wonder if there is such a thing we call equality. Jesus said, "Go into the vineyard and work and whatsoever is right I will pay." Sometimes whatsoever is right is not always equal. It is relative. Equal to whom or what? I thought about this a long time and came to the conclusion that the boss can work less and get more pay and I can work more and get less pay because the position makes the difference. Bishop Fulton J. Sheen asks the question, "Is woman attaining her full dignity by insisting on equality, or should she be insisting on equity?" Equity is the perfection of equality, not its substitute. It has the advantage which equality does not have, of recognizing the specific differences between men and women. As a matter of fact, men and women are not equal in sex. They are not equal because they complement each other.

Some truth from the article "Is There a Superior Sex?" by Jo Durden-Smith and Diana DeSimone will shed some light on our discussion here.[24]

Is There a Superior Sex?
Men and Women are Physically Different

1. Men and women differ in every cell of their bodies. This difference in the chromosome combination is the basic cause of the development into maleness or femaleness as the case may be.

2. Women have greater constitutional vitality, perhaps because of this chromosome difference. Normally, they outlive men by three or four years in the U.S.

3. The sexes differ in their basal metabolism—that of a woman being normally lower than that of a man.

4. They differ in skeletal structure, women having a shorter head, broader face, chin less protruding, shorter legs, and longer trunk. The first finger of a woman's hand is usually longer than the third; with men the reverse is true. Boys' teeth last longer than do those of girls.

5. A woman has larger stomach, kidneys, liver, and appendix, and has smaller lungs.

6. In functions, women have several important ones totally lacking in men—menstruation, pregnancy, and lactation. All of these influence behavior and feelings. They have more different hormones than do men. The same gland behaves differently in the two sexes—thus woman's thyroid is larger and more active; it enlarges during pregnancy but also during menstruation; it makes her more prone to goiter, provides resistance to cold and is associated with smooth skin, a relatively hairless body, and a thin layer of subcutaneous fat which are important elements in the concept of personal beauty. It also contributes to emotional instability—she laughs and cries more easily.

7. Women's blood contains more water (20% fewer red cells). Since these supply oxygen to the body cells, she tires more easily and is more prone to faint. Her constitutional viability is therefore strictly a long-range matter. When the working day in British factories, under wartime

conditions was increased from 10 to 12 hours, accidents of women increased 150%, of men not at all.

8. In brute strength, men are above women.

9. A woman's heart beats more rapidly (80 vs. 72 for men); blood pressure (10 points lower than men) varies from minute to minute; but she has much less tendency to high blood pressure at least until after menopause.

10. Her vital capacity of breathing power is lower in the 7:10 ratio.

11. She stands high temperature better than does man; metabolism slows down less.

The Wife's Responsibility for Oneness
Men and Women are Different Mentally and Psychologically

1. Verbal and spatial abilities in boys tends to be 'packaged' into different hemispheres: the right   hemisphere for nonverbal tasks, the left for verbal tasks. But in girls nonverbal skills are likely to be found on both sides of the brain. This affects their actions and reactions.

2. From shortly after birth, females are more sensitive to certain types of sounds, particularly the mother's voice, but also to loud noises.

3. Girls have more skin sensitivity, particularly in the finger-tips, and are more proficient at fine motor performance.

4. Girls are more attentive to social contexts—faces, speech patterns, and subtle vocal cues.

5. Girls speak sooner, have larger vocabularies, rarely demonstrate speech defects, exceed boys in language abilities, and learn foreign languages more easily.

6. Boys show early visual superiority.

7. Boys have better total body coordination but are poor at detailed activity; e.g. stringing beads.

8. Boys have different "attentional mechanisms" and react as quickly to inanimate objects as to a person.

9. Boys are more curious about exploring the environment.

10. Boys are better at manipulating three-dimensional space. They can mentally rotate or fold an object better.

11. Of eleven subtests for psychological measurements in the most widely used general intelligence test, only two (digit span and picture arrangement) reveal similar means scans for males and females. There are six differences so constant that the standard battery of this intelligence test now contains a masculinity-femininity index to offset sex-related proficiencies and deficiencies.

12. Girls who are assertive and active and can control events have greater intellectual development, while these factors are not as significant in male intellectual development.

13. More boys are hyperactive. (More than 90% of hyperactive people are males.)

14. Because the male brain is primarily visual and learns by manipulating its environment, listing instruction for boys in early elementary grades is more stressful for them. Girls therefore tend to exceed them.

15. Girls do less well on scholarship tests that are more geared for male performance at higher grades.

I found additional information concerning differences between men and women in an article by Dr. Paul Popenoe in Family Life magazine.[25]

Are Women Really Different?

1. The woman's immune system is more complex. She produces more immunoglobulen M. Her estrogen protects her from heart disease.

2. Males have a greater infant mortality rate.

   a) More males are spontaneously aborted and are born dead.

   b) 30% more males die within the first month of life.

   c) 3% more males have birth defects.

   d) 5 times as many males have language disability and stutter.

3. Females mature faster than males.

4. Females are chemically and biologically adapted to child bearing and raising.

5. Males are more chemically and biologically adapted to hunting and providing.

Finally, data gathered by Dr. Richard Restak, a neurologist at Georgetown University School of Medicine revealed the following differences:

1. In women, the left hemisphere of the brain is better developed. Therefore:

   a) She has better verbal and communication skills.

   b) She is more sensitive and context-oriented.

   c) She is two times more susceptible to phobias and is more prone to depression because she has less control from the right hemisphere of the brain.

2. In a man, the right hemisphere of the brain is better developed. Therefore:

   a) He is better at visual, spatial, mathematics, and abstract manipulations.

   b) He is a thinker and explorer.

   c) He is more sex-oriented and tends to establish "turf."

   d) He commits almost all-violent crimes and more men are sex deviants and psychopaths because they have less control from the left hemisphere of their brains.

3. Women have greater individual mood fluctuations. One in four women are seriously affected in pre-menstruation. Also at this time, women are inclined toward more illness, more tension, and show more inclination to crime.

4. There are more males at both ends of the intellectual spectrum—more retarded as well as more geniuses.

Once we understand and accept that these differences exist, we can get along with each other better in relationships. Our expectations can be framed better around what we know about the opposite sex and we will be more accepting of each other's differences, strengths, and weaknesses.

Force #3: Failure to Anticipate Selfishness

The failure to anticipate selfishness in marriage threaten oneness. Everyone has a natural tendency to be self-centered and destructive in relationships. The Bible tells us about our tendency to selfishness.

> As it is written, There is none righteous, no, not one: There is none that understandeth, there is none that seeketh after God. They are all gone out of the way, they are together become unprofitable; there is none that doeth good, no, not one. Their throat is an open sepulchre; with their tongues they have used deceit; the poison of asps

is under their lips: Whose mouth is full of cursing and bitterness: Their feet are swift to shed blood: Destruction and misery are in their ways: And the way of peace have they not known: There is no fear of God before their eyes. (Romans 3:10–19)

O wretched man that I am! who shall deliver me from the body of this death? (Romans 7:24)

All we like sheep have gone astray; we have turned every one to his own way; and the LORD hath laid on him the iniquity of us all. (Isaiah 53:6)

Our culture today promotes and encourages selfishness. Think of the commercial for a popular candy bar. The candy separates into several pieces and can easily be shared with a friend. However, the commercial makes fun of the fact that even though it can be easily divided, purchasers of the candy love it so much, they refuse to share. The slogan is, "Two for me, none for you."

Because we marry with stars in our eyes, we cannot see the reality of selfishness in our loved one. During dating, there is usually little daily responsibility and pressure, and both parties are trying to put their best foot forward. Early in the relationship, appreciation and approval are freely reflected. As the relationship progresses, selfishness makes us focus on our mate's weaknesses. Then, as we reflect disappointment and disapproval, our mate will become fearful, feel rejected and discouraged and this will result in lower performance. Our selfish nature seeks to justify our rejections of our mate.

Recognize this tendency toward selfishness in yourself and in your mate and be ready for it when it manifests.

Force #4: Failure to Work Through Inevitable Difficulties and Trials

A failure to work through inevitable difficulties and trials threatens oneness in marriage. There is a failure to accept the certainty of difficulties and problems. God will allow difficulties in your life for many reasons. For example, they trying of your faith builds patience.

Knowing this, that the trying of your faith worketh patience. But let patience have her perfect work, that ye may be perfect and entire, wanting nothing. (James 1:3–4)

Two blessings of perfect patience are:

1. Personal perfection in the knowledge of the Gospel and the will of God, and

2. Personal completeness in all the graces and gifts of God.

In your marriage, when your faith is tried or tested, there is really only one thing for you to do: Be patient and wait to see how God is going to work things out. Difficulties should force you to your knees and into the Word of God. Once there, you will experience the first blessing of discovering the will of God by coming into a more perfected knowledge of His word. Then, as deliverance happens, whether you are delivered from the trial or carried through it, God's grace and the gifts will be in evident operation and there is that second blessing that comes from perfect patience.

One young couple hit a financial snag in their marriage. The difficulty drew them closer to God. They began standing on God's word and realizing the truth of the fact that they had never seen the righteous forsaken. They continued to tithe and trust God because they knew that was His will. God's grace was evident to them in many ways during this time, not the least of which was the fact that they never went hungry. One day, another family just showed up with nine bags of groceries for them. Their patience had been perfected through their trial.

Force #5: An Extramarital Affair for Fulfillment Outside of Marriage

An extramarital affair is an escape from reality. A sexual love affair is an attempt to receive fulfillment outside of marriage. Who ever promised you total fulfillment and complete happiness in every area of your life? We are deceived into believing that we deserve complete fulfillment and perfect happiness, so extramarital affairs take many different forms. There's the love affair, the career affair, the materialism affair, the activities affair, and the apathy affair. Any one of these will destroy oneness in marriage.

If you hearken back to the Lynch mentality, it's easy to see how this force can infiltrate the American household. The love affair happens because it has been ingrained in the man that he exists to bring sexual pleasure to as many women as possible. He steps out on his wife and is applauded by his buddies who have bought into the same lie. Once the affair is discovered, the marriage is ruined.

The career affair can easily happen when the American man or woman finally breaks into a valued career. He or she has struggled through college and has worked his or her way up the corporate ladder, fighting against all kinds of pressure along the way. Once the position is achieved, he or she justifies the long hours with the necessity to hold the job that was so hard to get in the first place. All the while, the family is being neglected because he or she has become a workaholic. The marriage is ruined.

The materialism affair takes place when the person reaches a certain level of financial gain and begins to acquire "things". These "things" take on more of a meaning than their actual function. Lots of appliances, for example, means more than "I am efficient in the kitchen" and takes on the meaning "I no longer have to be a slave to my kitchen." The appliances define the person and give the person value. This warped way of looking at possessions can ruin the marriage.

The activities affair happens when the American man or woman feels compelled to run from function to function in an effort to prove worth. For so long, being a part of professional organizations for example has been denied to certain professionals. Now that the doors are open, they feel an obligation to become members in good standing to prove that they are just as good as anyone else in the profession. However, these activities take away from vital family time, and again, can lead to the ruin of the marriage.

Finally, the apathy affair hits the family when the couple feels it's just not worth it to try anymore. The expression of apathy becomes a living, breathing drive and, as ironic as it sounds, lots of energy is spent being apathetic. Since it is natural to respond positively to the one you love, the apathy affair forces the person to have to work hard at not caring. The more apathetic one party gets, the harder the other one tries to overcome the apathy, and the struggle between the two becomes intense. The very attention the apathetic party gets is what keeps the apathy fueled. Finally, the caring party gives up and the apathy affair has won. Marriage ruined.

Part Two:
Five Phases of Marriage Deterioration

Once any one of the five forces that destroy oneness and cause isolation in marriage is allowed to take hold, the marriage can begin to deteriorate. There are five phases of marriage deterioration.

Phase #1: The Romantic Phase

The first phase of marital deterioration begins before you even realize it. It happens during dating or during the honeymoon. This phase is built, not on something that you do, but on something that you don't do. During the romantic phase, the oneness and happiness of both people in the marriage is your goal, however, you do not have a plan as to how you will achieve this goal. The social, physical, and emotional relationship is an incomplete picture of marriage. Intense feelings characterize this phase, but there is not plan to sustain these feelings.

Phase #2: The Transition Phase

During the honeymoon or early marriage, a couple begins to make adjustments to each other in their values, habits, and expectation. If disappointments happen, they strike the heart, but are either quickly extinguished by overwhelming feelings for each other, or they are ignored.

Phase #3: The Reality Phase

Now the relationship begins to take on new dimensions as the following press in against it:

- Moving to an unfamiliar environment
- Establishing new friendships
- Job changes and stress

- Conflicting material values

- Children and parenting issues

- Parental and in-law expectations and interference

- Conflicting financial philosophies

- The realities of life sober the relationship, and feelings begin to vary greatly.

There's a struggle to change and meet these new demands. Disappointment sets in and discouragement begins to dominate the relationship.

Phase #4: The Retaliation Phase

Emotional and even physical retaliation becomes an alternative. Resentment and bitterness begin to take their toll. A man sells his life out to his profession or interests outside of the home. The woman pours her life into the children, seeks social identity outside the home, or seeks a new career. The marriage is no longer viewed with expectancy, but with despair.

Phase #5: The Rejection Phase

The death of a relationship happens when two alternatives are clearly seen. First, there is emotional separation and withdrawal. When emotional separation takes place, the relationship dies. Second, there is physical separation which could lead to divorce.

The heart is so hardened against the relationship that even the known consequences and the unknown future are overridden by hostility or discouragement.

The consequences of marital deterioration hurts everybody. This progression of marital failure leads to oppressive and disastrous circumstances for families and for the nation. Society becomes a group of aimless, discouraged, and isolated people. Little leadership is developed for the church, business, and society. Children suffer from an extreme lack of family models. Men cannot experience love and respect, though they may be highly successful. Women cannot experience love and appreciation, though they appear outwardly beautiful. And, the next generation experiences the results of the deteriorating family.

PART THREE:
EIGHT CAUSES OF FAMILY BREAKDOWN

In addition to the five forces that destroy oneness in marriage and lead to isolation, and the five phases of marriage deterioration, according to Tim and Bev LaHaye, there are eight causes for today's family breakdown.

1. Dominance of atheistic, anti-Christian humanism in the schools and media.

2. Immorality and promiscuity. (Nothing is more devastating to a marriage and home than infidelity.)

3. Legalization of pornography.

4. Women in the work force. Since World War I, women in the work force has increased from 2 percent to perhaps 49 percent of married women. This puts an abnormal temptation before both sexes. It is quite common for married couples to spend more working hours a week in a close relationship with someone else's spouse than with their own. Many cannot resist this temptation. One of the current fads is the renting of motel rooms for two-hour lunch breaks.

5. Easy divorce. According to Alvin Toffer, "The modern 'throw-away' marriage makes divorce easy." Ever since the courts recognized the no-fault divorce with only a six-month waiting period, marital break-ups have increased alarmingly. A judge once said in his opinion, one-third of all divorces he granted could have been avoided if the couple had sought the counsel of their party instead of his courtroom.

6. The permissive philosophy of the last generation. The non-Biblical child-raising concepts of Dr. Benjamin Spock and his followers—who announced that permissivism encouraged creativity, and thus a child should be given the right to express himself—have proven a dismal failure. They have produced a whole generation of selfish, inconsiderate, undisciplined

adults, too immature ever to marry, but who do so anyway. They reject, abuse, or abandon their children and when the going gets tough, they bail out. Dr. Spock admitted his mistake back in 1974, advocating that parents return to disciplining their children. Unfortunately, this retraction was too late for some who have had a genuine conversion to Christ followed by a desire to establish their home environment and child treatment on Biblical principles, yet who are facing a society that has been influenced by his early teaching to think the opposite.

7. Urbanized man. From all over the world, people are migrating toward the city. Somehow man believes that his fortune will be found in the next big city, so he leaves his homeland or base, relatives, and friends, and takes up a whole new way of life. This produces families with minimal roots and an absence of established social morals.

8. The women's lib morality. In the name of rights for women, a whole new lifestyle is creeping into America's family domain, one that is weakening the father's role in the home at the expense of the marriage and the family. Feminine-dominated homes are on the increase at an alarming rate. The irony of it is that American women already have better rights than do women in any other country of the world. The Equal Rights Amendment could

be a tragedy if it ever passes the required number of state legislatures. In the name of equal employment opportunities, it might open the door to a rise in unemployment and the discontinuance of alimony and child support. Another irony is that the ERA will probably not provide one woman a single employment opportunity or right that is not already guaranteed by the portions of the Civil Rights Acts already passed by the U.S. Congress. But the ERA will contribute to the breakdown of the home. Careerism for women has already brought many to the point of conflict between commitment to a career and a commitment to motherhood. Science has made it possible for women to prevent conception or delay having children so long that it becomes physically dangerous to have them at all.

Chapter Ten

What God Hath Joined Together

One of the most important decisions we will ever have to make in life is having to choose a life-long partner. With such a momentous and far-reaching decision, we really need divine wisdom.

Proverbs 3:5–6 says, "Trust in the Lord with all thine heart and lean not unto thine own understanding. In all thy ways acknowledge Him and He shall direct thy paths." Now this particular scripture does not advocate passive praying. It says to at least have a plan of action, thinking of ways to achieve your goals.

It says *in all your ways* acknowledge Him and He shall direct your paths. Sometimes we think we know it all, we try to be self-contained, not needing any advice or divine assistance and thus we make many mistakes. Proverbs 3:7 says, "Be not wise in thine own eyes." When it comes to deciding on a wife, a husband or any other decisions; job, church, city, we had better seek divine wisdom.

Every sincere Christian wants to know, "How can I really know the will of God for my life?" But sometimes we imagine God's hand in a situation. For example, a certain man is praying for God's guidance in choosing a wife. While praying, the telephone rings and it just happens to be a girl calling to ask him a question about a college lab assignment. The man decides that God is answering his prayers by allowing the girl to call him at that specific moment. He believes that these simultaneous experiences are God's way of doing things. To him, this is God's way of saying, "This is the girl I have picked out for you." The courtship begins, he proposes marriage soon afterwards and is crushed later when he finds out that they were never compatible. Did God join them together? I don't think so!

God has a revealed will for all people in a general sense and an unrevealed will for everyone in specific situations. His revealed will is called His universal will for us. This will governs His desires for all human beings. Therefore, just as our parents desire the best for us, so does God the Father. God's universal will allows individual decisions to be made. We have the Ten Commandments, the Beatitudes, and the Epistles of Paul. As long as your choices do not violate scripture in any point, you have leverage and room for your own decisions.

God has not revealed the specific decisions we have to make to remain within His will. God's not going to say to you, "Choose Mary or Janie." I don't believe the idea of "one and only" decisions and God having a blueprint for our lives are found in the New Testament. I don't believe there's just one person in the whole world with whom we could be happily married or just one occupation for each of us in order to remain within God's will. God is not playing a game of "hide-and-go-seek" with us. He does not have hidden somewhere just one choice for us to discover. Sometimes the wife or the husband dies. If they were the only ones, then the widow or widower could never marry again. God makes many fish in the sea and many of everything. He has lots of good wives and husbands. You've known them when you've seen them. That is the reason I say that you can be married to a Who and not a What. The husband is a What, the wife is a What, and *what* God hath joined together let no man put asunder.

Dating is a prolonged interview to determine whether or not you've found Mr. or Mrs. Right and vice versa. We reserve the right to refuse, based upon the data ascertained during the dating period. Never make premature decisions. But on the other hand, it shouldn't take very long to make a decision when you know what your values are.

We should not look for ways to detour the use of our minds in making choices about the particular decisions in our lives. God designed our minds, and when we don't use them, we are despising His design. Christianity is not a mindless religion. To reject the use of the mind is to fail at the beginning point of Christianity. "Love the Lord your God with . . . all your mind," (Matthew 22:37 NIV). God created our minds so that He could reveal content to us, but not to reveal every minute decision we should make. We become robots when we do not use our minds. We are denying ourselves the humanity God has given to us. In Christ, God renewed our minds so that they could be used in His service (Romans 12:12). God did not create us to function as automatic machines or to act out of mere instinct as animals do. We were created with the ability to think, rationalize, decipher, weigh, and make intelligent decisions as well as to act upon the basis of those decisions.

Should I marry? If so to whom? Remember the man praying for a mate and the telephone ringing at the same time and he thought that God was telling him that was the one for him? God has not left us with a shaky method such as "simultaneous experiences" as the basis for discovering our mates. The principle is universal will. Is marriage within the boundaries of God's universal will? Yes.

Godly Characteristics

Can you express God's characteristics in your reason for wanting to marry or in your choice of a potential mate? Are you marrying someone because of his or her financial status? Can your potential mate's talents aid in your personal advancement in some way? Are you selecting a mate out of revenge toward someone who "dropped" you, or perhaps out of rebellion against your parents?

Consider the following general Biblical principles concerning marriage:

1. Do not marry a non-Christian.

2. Your mate should be a helper fit for you.

3. A successful marriage rests upon leaving parents, cleaving to your mate and becoming one flesh (Genesis 2:24).

Does this person complete the areas of your life in which you are lacking? Does he or she bring balance to your life? In my marriage, my wife completes me in all of the areas of my life that are void or lacking. Do you complement one another? A person cannot realistically marry everyone who is nice, but should marry a person who is a balance to selfhood and one whose life he or she can complement or complete.

I hear people say when they are looking for a life-long partner and friend, "I just can't seem to find the right one." My question to them is, "Are *you* the right one looking for the right one? Can *you* complete or complement the right one? Are *you* the What for the What?" You must be a giver as well as a receiver in marriage. The husband and the wife must be an asset and not a liability; and they should help and not hinder one another.

Are you ready for the adjustments of leaving father and mother? Can you cut the apron strings upon leaving? Can you devote yourself to your spouse so that no interests can come between the two of you (cleaving)? Do you share the same purpose and life goals (one flesh)? Are you ready to remain with your mate, come what may, until death separates you? (Romans 7:2, 1 Corinthians 7:39) Now that you've answered all of the preliminary questions, let's focus on some other important issues.

Counsel

Have the two of you sought wise counsel from others? I was at a health spa with a friend of mine in North Carolina, discussing the subject of this book when a young man in his 30's heard the conversation as I began to state some things concerning a good wife and the church. He interrupted and commented, "I married a woman in the church and it was the worst mistake of my life." He also admitted that he refused the counsel of a renowned and wise minister. During the counseling session, the minister asked the young lady what she believed marriage was all about. She replied that marriage should be a 50/50 relationship and so forth.

The minister later met with the young man alone and warned him, "Brother, you will be making a mistake if you marry that young lady." He refused the minister's counsel and married the lady anyway.

The young man admitted that no matter what he did to try and please her, it did not work. And everything he wanted to do to fulfill his life's dream, she worked totally against him, as if his dreams meant nothing to her. He gladly said that he eventually ended up having to divorce this young woman.

Now this young man is not a bum or a derelict. He is an entrepreneur, a school teacher, and he drives a Mercedes and a Porsche. Then he said that after his divorce, he dated twenty other women and could not find one who seemed to be the right one for him. This young man comes from a middle class home of the 1950's, his mother and father are both Christians and raised him in the church. He began to reflect upon the marital relationship of his mother and father and remembered the way his mother took care of his dad and desired the same kind of woman for himself. He has a 1950's perception of marriage, but was married to a 1990's woman. How can the two walk together except they agree? (Amos 3:3.) Jesus said, "A house that is divided against itself cannot stand (Matthew 12:25).

A Little Common Sense

Do you really know the person you're thinking about marrying? I have heard of love at first sight and people have gotten married within two weeks, or even one or two days, of first meeting each other. I don't recommend that at all because it takes time to get to know that other person. As I said before, dating is like a pro-longed interview. We need to ask probing questions. Dating can be thought of as a means for gathering data—facts or figures from which conclusions can be inferred.

Have you observed the other person in his or her home envi-ronment? Ladies, beware of any man that disrespects his mother. She is the first woman in his life and if he doesn't know how to love and respect the first one, then he will not know how to love and respect you either. On the other hand, men beware of any woman who does not know how to love and respect her father. (I am obviously not talking about low-down, dirty men who molest and abuse their children.) Remember that her father is the first man in her life and if she doesn't love and respect him, she will do you the same way.

I know a man who married a woman who did not get along with her father. Because her father was very domineering, she and her father would verbally fight all of the time. This taught her to resist all men. As a result, her marriage failed.

Just saying God has chosen this person for you is passive to say the least. Neither is it enough for you to "feel like" you are in love. You cannot base your marriage solely on the feeling of love; we fall in and out of love many times in a single lifetime.

But do take some feelings into consideration. God has given you intuition. How do you *really* feel about the person? Can you put him or her first? Are you satisfied with his or her proposed plans? Is there any faking or apprehension? Do you really want to get married?

Finally ask yourself, can you marry this person with the assurance that God will bless your union? Do not think there is just one person in the world who you can marry in order to receive God's blessing?

Let No Man Put Asunder
By Wayne Perryman—May 19, 1992

In Matthew 19:6, Jesus said what many ministers say today during wedding ceremonies, "What therefore God hath joined together, let no man put asunder." The question is this, are all Christian couples joined together by God? Many ministers avoid this question, but the answer is clearly, No! Although it is God who ordained the institution of marriage, he is not the one responsible for many of the marriages today. In other words there is nothing wrong with the act of marriage. It is a godly act. But who we marry can be a very ungodly act (Duet. 7:3). One person explained it this way, "There is nothing wrong with making a living. But there is something wrong if we do it by robbing the bank." God has never been against marriage, but he has been against marrying people he doesn't approve of. To further illustrate this point, perhaps we should ask the following:

1. Was it God who joined Ahab with Jezebel? (1 Kings 16:29–31)

2. Was it God who joined Hagar with Abraham? (Genesis 16:1–16)

3. Was it God who joined David with Bathsheba? (2 Samuel 11:2–12:13)

4. Was it God who joined Solomon with his 300 wives? (1 Kings 11:1–8)

> Are these the types of relationships God said, "Let no man put asunder?" I think not. What the scripture clearly says is, "What *God* has joined together," making a Divine distinction between God's match making skills vs. our own. The scripture does not say nor does it imply that God joins all couples together.[26]

Jewish Customs and Laws

The disciples once asked about divorce, making reference to Moses and the Jewish custom regarding marriage and divorce. When looking at Jesus' response in the proper context, we must keep in mind that with the Jewish custom, the man was the priest and head of his home, and one of his duties was to select a good godly Jewish wife for his son. The selection process for choosing the wife was considered to be as much a religious act as the wedding ceremony itself. So when the Jewish father selected the Jewish girl for his Jewish son, it was considered to have the endorsement of God (Genesis 24:42, 48 & 50).

Since their selection process and wedding ceremony was done in reverence to God, Jesus said as a seal of approval for their marriage custom, "let no man put asunder." In other words, the entire match-making process was done in reverence to God and with his endorsement. The Jewish marriage (when done properly) was all part of preserving and protecting Israel's covenant with God through Abraham. That's why Abraham would not let Isaac marry a Canaanite and chose a Jewish girl for him instead.

Modern customs of having the boy ask the girl's father for her hand in marriage are similar to this, but today men are not considered to be priests of their households and our selection of marriage partners is not done in reverence to God. Not only in our times, but throughout the Bible God has had problems with His people marrying people of whom He did not approve. (Ezra chapters 9 &10). In the tenth chapter of Ezra, the people were permitted to divorce their heathen wives because God did not approve of those marriages. Keep in mind, like many of us, these Jews married these women because of their good looks, not their godly lifestyles.

The People's Choice

What we often forget is that God gives us all the freedom of choice, and often our choice is not God's choice. We see evidence of this when Israel wanted a king. Saul was clearly their choice, not God's choice. They pleaded with Samuel, "Give us a king like all other nations have." Samuel was terribly upset and went to the Lord for advice.

"Do as they say," the Lord replied, "for I am the one they are rejecting, not you. They don't want me to be their king any longer. Ever since I brought them from Egypt they have continually forsaken Me and followed other gods. And now they are giving you the same treatment. Do as they ask, but warn them about what it will be like to have a king."

How many times have pastors tried to tell couples that they weren't right for each other or that he felt God would not approve of their marriage or that they shouldn't get married for other reasons, but the couples failed to listen to his advice and got married anyway? Do you think God joined these people together?

God's Match-Making Skills

Today, many feel if a person looks good and is sexy, then it must mean that the individual himself or herself is good. Saul's good looks and his fine-tuned body certainly didn't hurt his chances of becoming king (1 Samuel 9:2). Do you honestly believe Israel would have accepted him as king if Saul was short, fat, and ugly? No way! God knows that our selection and rejection process of choosing people is heavily influenced by a person's physical appearance. That's why in 1 Samuel 16:7, when selecting Israel's next king, God told Samuel to, ". . . look not on his countenance or on the height of his stature; because I have refused him: for the Lord seeth not as man seeth; for man looketh on the outward appearance, but the Lord looketh on the heart."

Although many people fall in love because of their mates' good looks and good bodies, this is not why God joins people in holy wedlock. God joins Christian couples together so their marriage (like our individual lives) will glorify Him. If a person marries someone of whom God has not approved, God's glorification cannot happen because God's glorification cannot evolve from disobedience. Disobedience itself is sin.

When a minister says, "What God has joined together let no man put asunder," this doesn't mean that God has brought the two together or that God himself has actually approved the marriage. God is very clear regarding the types of marriages he approves and disapproves. In 2 Corinthians 6:14, it says, "Be not unequally yoke together with unbelievers: for what fellowship hath righteousness with unrighteousness? And what communion hath light with darkness?" This lets us know that God does not approve marriages to non-Christians. So we know that Matthew 19:6 does not pertain to these type of marriages.

What the Christian church has failed to teach us, though, is that all Christians aren't compatible. Some Christians aren't meant to be together. When a young girl comes home and tells her parents that the young man she is interested in is a Christian so they don't have anything to worry about, what she doesn't realize is just because a person says he or she is a Christian doesn't mean that this person is approved by God for marriage.

In true Christian marriages, God determines who we should marry, not us. It is only in these God approved marriages that He commands that no man should put asunder. We see God's match-making skills in operation in Genesis the 24th chapter with Rebekah and Isaac and in Matthew with Mary and Joseph. According to Genesis 24:11, there were plenty of girls Isaac could have married, but God had selected Rebekah for him. God knew the two were made for each other.

Just because two people are both Christians isn't a guarantee that the two people are meant for each other, nor is it a green light to get married. This factor is commonly overlooked by young Christians who fall in love. Consider that Paul and Barnabus were not only Christians, they also had a good relationship. But while planning a missionary trip, they had a strong argument over John Mark in Acts 15:39. The scripture said their disagreement was so sharp that they decided they shouldn't travel together and took separate trips. This is very important to know because most people think if two people are Christians, that's all that's required for a meaningful relationship. To the contrary, Christians have as many, if not more conflicts than non-Christians. This is not to say that good Christian marriages do not have conflict, but rather that those marriages that aren't approved by God are likely to have more than what is considered normal for a healthy relationship. Although conflicts are a natural part of any relationship, relationships that lack compatibility are bound to have more than their share.

Even though the scripture tells us not to be unequally yoked together, this doesn't mean that people obey or honor this commandment. In Deuteronomy 22:10 it says, "Thou shalt not plow with an ox and an ass (yoked) together." Even though this was the law, some people still violated the law. One may ask, "Why wouldn't Israel want these two animals together, since both are known for their ability to plow?" I would say for the same reason God wouldn't want us with someone whose character and beliefs are not compatible with our own. If we look at the character of the donkey and the ox, we will find that one is known for its stubbornness and the other is known for its bullheadedness. What a combination! Wasn't God right on point to choose those two animals to illustrate just how many of the marriages today turn out that are put together by man?

Let's take the statement, "be not unequally yoked together" and add Amos 3:3, which says, "how can two walk together except they agree?" And if we can see these two statements to mean not only having the same Christian faith but overall compatibility as well, we will have a better understanding of the types of people God will bring together. This is not to say opposites don't attract or that a couple God brings together will agree on everything. I sincerely believe God brings a person in our life who will complement our weakness. Even so, the two parties must be

compatible as stated in 1 Corinthians 1:10, ". . . I plead with you
to be of one mind, united in thought and purpose" (Living);—
(Also see Phil. 1:27, 2 Cor. 13:11, and 1 Peter 3:8).

Compatibility Check List

In determining compatibility, couples who are thinking about
marriage should consider the following:

1. Are our backgrounds and cultures similar? If so, in what
   ways? If not, there may be some compatibility problems.

2. What type of church is this person used to? For instance,
   if one mate is from a Pentecostal church that believes in
   divine healing, speaking in tongues, dancing in the spirit,
   and the fasting and prayer approach to problem solving,
   but the other has never had this type of Christian experience, there may be some compatibility problems.

3. Who should be the head of the household and what does
   this mean to both parties? For instance, if one believes
   the man is the head of the household and the woman
   has no voice, but the other disagrees, there will be some
   compatibility problems.

4. What role should each person play in the relationship?
   If the roles in the relationship roles aren't defined and
   clear, there may be some compatibility problems.

5. How should children be disciplined? If one believes more in spanking than other forms of discipline, there may be some compatibility problems.

6. Who should manage the money in the household and what should be the financial priorities? If there is not a clear understanding of financial responsibilities and priorities, there may be some compatibility problems.

7. How should problem solving be handled? If one person believes in bringing in a third party like a family member or a friend and the other person wants to keep things in the immediate family only, there may be some compatibility problems.

8. How much social activity is enough? And what types of social activities are necessary for a healthy relationship? If one believes in just sitting in front of the TV watching sports and the other wants to get out and do things, there may be some compatibility problems.

9. How important is the bible in guiding their everyday life? If one person is used to looking to the Bible for answers and the other is not, there may be some compatibility problems.

10. Is each person ministry oriented? If so, what is their ministry? If this is not discussed and understood, there may be some compatibility problems.

11. What about tithing to the church? If one mate believes in tithing to ministries and the other doesn't, there may be some compatibility problems.

12. What about attitudes toward sex? If one person believes sex is for producing children only and sex for pleasure is sin, but the other mate disagrees, there may be some compatibility problems.

How important is compatibility? Barbara DeAngelis, Ph.D., author of *Are You the One for Me?* says, "The sad truth is, very few relationships end because the two partners do not love each other: they end because they are not compatible partners. . . ."

If God Didn't Join Us

What if we are both Christians but never discussed these areas of our lives before we got married? What if we are having problems and are convinced that God did not join us together? Should we get a divorce? In 1 Corinthians 7:12–16, Paul lets us know that what he is saying in these scriptures isn't from the Lord, it is his own opinion. In addition, the situation he refers to in these scripture passages pertains more to two people who originally weren't Christians, then if one becomes a Christian after they're married. Paul's opinion doesn't necessarily cover the situation in the question above—of two people who were Christians from the beginning, but never should have married each other in the first place.

My advice would be to pray, seek God, and talk to the pastor or a Christian counselor right away and this time listen to their wise counsel. In doing so, keep in mind that the best of Christian marriages, joined by God himself, also have problems, pressures, and their low points. That's why God said when these hardships come, He wants no man to (put asunder or) touch these relationships. When marriages are going well, no one thinks of divorce; it's only when times are bad that divorce is considered. God knows Satan will always attack Godly relationships, that's Satan's job (1 Peter 5:8). But God's job is to keep His marriages together (St. John 10:10). By keeping them together, these marriages can bring Him honor and glory. We must always keep in mind, that when a marriage totally relies on the Lord for its success (Psalms 127:1), it is literally impossible for Satan to destroy them (Matthew 19:26).

Spiritual Significance

The scripture tells us that God is a spirit and they that worship Him must worship Him in spirit and in truth (St. John 4:24). So everything He tells us has a spiritual significance, including the statement, "What God has joined together . . ." Again, when Christ made this statement, He was talking to the Jews in reference to their marriage customs. The Jewish marriage custom was approved by God for His chosen people and was God's method of joining the Jews together in holy wedlock. Let's look at three key components of the Hebrew marriage custom and how God used them to solidify their marriages.

1. The process of God joining two together includes God's command for children to "honor their father and mother." In the Hebrew custom, the children were permitted to marry as early as 12 or 13 years of age. Regardless of the age, the parents were very involved in selecting the spouse for their child (See Genesis 21:21 in which Ishmael's mother, Hagar, picks his wife for him. Also see Genesis 24 and Genesis 29). Every act of a Jewish child, including marriage, was to fulfill this commandment of God to bring honor to the parents. Christian marriages today that are truly joined by God will also comply with this commandment as well. The couples' parents will be (or should be) honored by the union of the two.

2. "What God hath joined together" includes the recognition of the father as the head of the family. In Genesis 3:16, God tells the woman that her husband "shall rule over her." In the Hebrew custom, not only did the father help select the mate for his child, he also had the final say on who the child could marry and when the child could marry. Today, Christians who want to be joined by God in holy wedlock should ask their heavenly Father as to who they should marry and when they should marry. The scripture in Proverbs 3:5–6, "Trust in the Lord with

all thine heart: and lean not unto thine own understanding, in all thy ways acknowledge Him and He shall direct thy path." If you did not ask God as to who you should marry—and wait for His answer—it is possible that you and your mate weren't joined together by God. Don't fret, remember, acknowledgment of wrong doing and repentance changes and corrects everything, even wrong marriages. Repentance worked for David and Bathsheba's wrong marriage and it can work for you. (2 Samuel 12:13–20).

3. What God hath joined together includes faith preservation. God instructed Israel not to marry heathens (as they did in Ezra the ninth chapter) because the heathens would have the tendency to draw Israel away from God. Today the heathen could be anyone who can come between you and your faith and your relationship with God. God will not join a person together with another if He feels the union will destroy or adversely affect their relationship with Him. Since God made all people and knows their heart, only He or His spiritual representative (pastor) can make such a determination.

When God joins people together in marriage, it is for their spiritual well-being and for no other purpose. Nothing else matters to God (Matthew 16:26 and Matthew 5:29). The decision to marry (for Christians) must rest on a spiritual foundation, and all three of the components above must be factored into the marriage process, especially component number two—dealing with asking our Heavenly Father whom He feels we should marry. These factors are vitally necessary if the couple wants to start off right by having God join them together in holy wedlock. By so doing, they can enter the marriage with the assurance and confidence of Roman 8:31 . . . "If God is for us, who can be against us."

In conclusion, like anyone else, Christians can get married without God's approval or involvement, and many do. These are clearly man-made marriages. (See Ezra 9:2&12.) Whatever man puts together, he becomes the god of it, according to John 10:34, and this authorizes him to take it apart, including marriages (See Ezra 10:2–11). These types of marriages are vulnerable and victims to third party influence. Studies show that a vast majority of the marriages today are broken up by the influence of third parties. But remember, in Matthew 19:6, Jesus is saying, "What therefore God hath joined together," He is the God of it and He, and He alone, has the authority to demand that, let no man, (and this includes judges, counselors, pastors, and relatives), put asunder. Keep in mind, when we see the beautiful world that God has created, we are reminded that there is a remarkable difference between what God puts together and what man puts together.

Finally, everything that happens in this world is not inspired by God, approved by God, condoned by God, or endorsed by God, including many of our marriages. Although He is blamed for many things, God has very little to do with many things that go on in this world. We often forget that according to John 12:31, Satan is the prince of this world and unfortunately the prince of many lives. Since he is in control of this world, it is essential that God be in control of our lives and decisions, and that includes the decision as to whom we should marry.

I firmly believe God would prefer that we divorce the attitudes and behaviors that cause marital problems rather than divorcing the people who are often classified as the problem. I'm convinced that if Christians fast and pray (the process that should have been used to select our mate in the first place), God will straighten out the problem His way, no matter what types of problems we may be facing, including wrong marriages or marriages that appear to be wrong. If we truly love God and turn all of our problems over to Him, Romans 8:28 says He can work "all things" out for the good. However, the Lord does recognize that some marriage partners may take on the lifestyle and attitude of an unbeliever, and with hardened hearts refuse to submit to the will of God. Paul said in 1 Corinthians 7:15, if they act this way and choose to leave the marriage, you may let them go and are no longer bound to them, "for God wants His children to live in peace and harmony." (TLB)

A Christian marriage is a total commitment of two people to each other and to the person of Jesus Christ. It involves vows taken before God, obeying scriptural teachings and references which pertain to Christians, a blessing and benediction from God upon the husband and wife, a time of testimony to their faith in Christ, a commitment to build their marriage upon biblical teachings, and a time of celebration and praise.

PREREQUISITES FOR BIBLICAL MARRIAGE – GENESIS 2:18, 24

1. **Help meet** – (compatibility) ". . . I will make him a helpmate for him" (Gen. 2:18).

2. **Leave** – (to abandon) "For this cause a man shall leave his father and his mother . . ."

3. **Cleave** – (forsake, to sever one relationship before establishing another) ". . . and shall cleave to his wife, and they shall become one flesh" (Matt. 19:5–6).

Conclusion

God intended loving order in the home. Once the balance is restored with man as the head and priest of the home and woman as the necessary helper, I believe families will become much stronger, and will see a drastic change in many of the social problems that plague our communities

I'd like to conclude with this excerpt from Watchman Nee's book entitled *Spiritual Authority.*[27]

> God is working towards recovering the oneness of the body. But for this to be accomplished there

must first be the life of the Head, followed next by
the authority of the Head. Without the life of the
Head there can be no body. Without the authority
of the Head there can be no unity of the body. To
maintain the oneness of the body we must let the
life of the Head rule.

In the Family

Wives, be in subjection unto your own husbands,
as unto the Lord. For the husband if the head of
the wife, as Christ also is the head of the
church...But as the church is subject to Christ, so
let the wives also be to their husbands in everything, (Ephesians 5:22-24).

Children, obey your parents in the Lord: for this is
right. Honor thy father and mother (which is the
first commandment with promise), that it may be
well with thee, and thou mayest live long on the
earth, (Ephesians 6:1-3).

Wives, be in subjection to your husbands, as is fit-
ting in the Lord...Children, obey your parents in
all things, for this is well-pleasing in the
Lord...Servants, obey in all things them that are
your masters according to the flesh; not with

eye-service, as men-pleasers, but in singleness of
heart, fearing the Lord, (Colossians 3:18, 20, 22).

God desires that we would obey His delegated authorities as
well as Himself. All the members of the body should be subject
to one another. When this is so, the body is one with itself and
with the Head. As the authority of the Head prevails, the will of
God is done. Thus does the church become the kingdom of God.

God sets up His authority in the home, but many of His children do not pay enough attention to this sphere of the family.
Yet the epistles, such as Ephesians and Colossians which are
considered the most spiritual letters, do not overlook this matter.
They specifically mention subjection in the home, that without
this there will be difficulty in the service of God. The letters of I
Timothy and Titus deal with the subject of work, but they also
speak of the family problem as being something which could
affect the work. Peter's first letter focuses on the kingdom, but
he too considers rebellion against familial authority as rebellion
against the kingdom. Once the members of a family see authority, many difficulties in the home will disappear.

God has set the husband as the delegated authority of Christ,
with the wife as representative of the church. It would be difficult for the wife to be subject to her husband if she did not see
the delegated authority vested in him by God. She needs to realize that the real issue is God's authority, not her husband. "That

they may train the young women to love their husbands, to love their children, to be sober-minded, chaste, workers at home, kind, being in subjection to their own husbands, that the word of God be not blasphemed," (Titus 2:4-5). "In like manner, ye wives, be in subjection to your own husbands; that, even if any obey not the word, they may without the word be gained by the behavior of their wives," (I Peter 3:1). "For after this manner aforetime the holy women, also who hoped in God, adorned themselves, being in subjection to their own husbands; as Sarah obeyed Abraham, calling him lord," (I Peter 3:5-6).

If we honor the authority of the Lord in our lives others will respect the Lord's authority in us.

Couples must begin to focus on the forces that exist that can ruin their marriage, adjust their awareness of each other, and set things straight in line with God's word. Once this happens, the barnyard will once again be a lovely place to live, grow, and thrive.

CONVERSION IS THE ANSWER

This conversion is "the birth of a new dominant affection." It is a change in belief, but it is more than that; it is a change in direction; it is a change in attitude, but more; at the basis it is a change of affection.

The conversion is a conversion of our Love. We have been loving self, sex, or the world supremely—now we love God supremely.

That Love is not a love place alongside other loves; it is a new dominant affection. It absorbs all lesser affections into itself and in the process frees them.

Conversion represents a reorientation of one's life and personality, which includes the adoption of a new ethical line of conduct, a forsaking sin and turning to righteousness.

Conversion—an altered understanding—an altered understanding of Christ.

Redemption is taking that which is useless and making it useful.

Endnotes

1. "Men: The Secret Victims of Domestic Violence," (Internet).

2. *Vines Expository Dictionary of Biblical Words* (Thomas Nelson Publishers).

3. Gary Thomas, "The Husband Abusers," *New Man Magazine* (April 1999).

4. Ken Abraham, *New Man Magazine* (May 1998).

5. Na'im Akbar, *Chains and Images of Psychological Slavery* (Jersey City, NJ: New Mind Productions, 1984), 7–27.

6. K. Clark and M. P. Clark, "The Development of Consciousness of Self and the Emergence of Racial Identification in Negro Pre-School Children," *Journal of Social Psychology* 591 (1939): 10.

7. William Lynch, "How to Make a Slave" (speech made in 1792, Internet).

8. *Matthew Henry's Commentary Volumn VI Acts to Revelation* (Old Tappen, NJ: Fleming H. Revell Company).

9. *Webster's New World Dictionary* (Simon Schuster, 1976, 1979).

10. Dick Bernal, *When Lucifer and Jezebel Join Your Church* (San Jose, CA: Jubilee Christian Center, 1994), 16, 47.

11. A. Frank Hammond and Ida Hammond, *Pigs in the Parlor* (Impact Books, Inc., 1973), 23, 24.

12. Win Worley, *Christians Can and Do Have Demons* (Lansing, IL: WRW Publications, 1990), 8, 9.

13. Ted W. Engstrom and Robert Larson, *Intergrity* (Waco, TX: Word Books Publisher, 1987), 37, 38.

14. *Church of God in Christ: Official Manual* (Memphis, TN: Church of God in Christ Publishing House, 1973), 144.

15. Tim LaHaye and Bev LaHaye, *The Spirit Controlled Family* (Old Tappen, NJ: Fleming H. Revell Company, 1978), 31, 32, 96.

16. E. Stanley Jones, *The Way* (Garden City, NY: Doubleday Company, Inc., 1978), 101.

17. T. D. Jakes, *The Lady, Her Lover, and Her Lord* (New York, NY: G. P. Putnam's Sons Publishers, 1998), 75, 76.

18. Patricia R. Gaddis, *Battered But Not Broken* (Judson Press, 1996).

19. Keith Intrater, *Covenant Relationships* (Shippensburg, PA: Destiny Image Publishers, 1989), 189, 190.

20. David Augsburger, *Caring Enough to Hear and Be Heard* (Ventura, CA: Regal Books, 1982), 6, 7.

21. Barbara De Angelis, *Are You the One for Me?* (New York, NY: Bantam Doubleday Dell Publishing Group, 1992), 157, 196.

22. T. Garrolt Benjamin, Jr., *Boys to Men* (Indianapolis, IN: Heaven on Earth Publishing House, 1993), 45–48.

23. J. Vernon McGee, *Marriage and Divorce* (Nashville, TN: Thomas Nelson Publishers, 1998), 37, 38.

24. Jo Durden-Smith and Diana Desimone, "Is There a Superior Sex?" Readers Digest (Nov. 1982).

25. Paul Popenoe, *Family Life* (Feb. 1971): 17–22.

26. Wayne Perryman, *Let No Man Put Asunder* (Consultants Confidential of Mercer Island, WA, May 1992), 82–90.

27. Watchman Nee, *Spiritual Authority* (New York, NY: Christian Fellowship Publishers, Inc., 1972), 54, 65, 67.

28. Rosie Milligan, *Satisfying the Black Man Sexually* (Los Angeles, CA: Professional Business Consultants), 520.

To order additional copies of

TROUBLE IN THE BARNYARD

Call (800)917-BOOK

or send $14.95 + $3.95 shipping and handling to

Books Etc.
P.O. Box 4888
Seattle, WA 98104